Praxis
Early Childhood Education Practice Questions

Dear Future Exam Success Story

First of all, **THANK YOU** for purchasing Mometrix study materials!

Second, congratulations! You are one of the few determined test-takers who are committed to doing whatever it takes to excel on your exam. **You have come to the right place.** We developed these practice tests with one goal in mind: to deliver you the best possible approximation of the questions you will see on test day.

Standardized testing is one of the biggest obstacles on your road to success, which only increases the importance of doing well in the high-pressure, high-stakes environment of test day. Your results on this test could have a significant impact on your future, and these practice tests will give you the repetitions you need to build your familiarity and confidence with the test content and format to help you achieve your full potential on test day.

Your success is our success

We would love to hear from you! If you would like to share the story of your exam success or if you have any questions or comments in regard to our products, please contact us at **800-673-8175** or **support@mometrix.com**.

Thanks again for your business and we wish you continued success!

Sincerely,
The Mometrix Test Preparation Team

TABLE OF CONTENTS

Practice Test #1

Language Arts

1. When very young children begin to produce idiomorphs, this is part of which stage of oral language development?
   - a. The Cooing stage
   - b. The One-Word stage
   - c. The Telegraphic stage
   - d. The Babbling stage

2. One ECE student's parents want to know if their child is gifted. Another student's parents want to know if their child has a developmental disability. A third student's parents want to know how well their child is mastering all areas of development. A fourth student's parents want to know if and how their child's mastery levels may have changed since last year. What kinds of tests should the educators give the children to answer these parents' questions?
   - a. Norm-referenced tests for the first and third child, criterion-referenced for the second and fourth
   - b. Norm-referenced tests for the first two children, and criterion-referenced tests for the other two
   - c. Criterion-referenced tests for the first two children, and norm-referenced tests for the other two
   - d. Criterion-referenced tests for the first and third child, norm-referenced for the second and fourth

3. Print awareness skills typically demonstrated independently by preschoolers include:
   - a. Recognizing printed letters, but not necessarily also printed words.
   - b. Reciting the alphabet, but not identifying single letters in isolation.
   - c. Recognizing printed words, but not using these for communicating.
   - d. Reciting ABCs; recognizing letters and words; print communication.

4. A teacher asks her students to say the word *map*. She then says, "Change the /m/ sound to a /t/ sound. What word do you have now?" Which phonemic awareness skill are students practicing?
   - a. Alliteration
   - b. Segmenting
   - c. Blending onset and rime
   - d. Phoneme substitution

5. All members of a group of kindergarten students early in the year are able to chant the alphabet. The teacher is now teaching the students what the alphabet looks like in written form. The teacher points to a letter and the students vocalize the correspondent sound. Alternatively, the teacher vocalizes a phoneme and a student points to it on the alphabet chart. The teacher is using _____ in her instruction.
   - a. letter–sound correspondence
   - b. rote memorization
   - c. predictive analysis
   - d. segmentation

6. A teacher is working with a group of third graders at the same reading level. Her goal is to improve reading fluency. She asks each child in turn to read a page from a book about mammal young. She asks the children to read with expression. She also reminds them they don't need to stop between each word; they should read as quickly as they comfortably can. She cautions them, however, not to read so quickly that they leave out or misread a word. The teacher knows the components of reading fluency are:

 a. Speed, drama, and comprehension
 b. Cohesion, rate, and prosody
 c. Understanding, rate, and prosody
 d. Rate, accuracy, and prosody

7. To determine the subject matter of a section within a text chapter, what should the teacher tell the student to do?

 a. Read the section heading
 b. Read the chapter glossary
 c. Read the index in the text
 d. Read through the section

8. Which of the following is true about the author's point of view or purpose in an informational text?

 a. Readers can always identify this because informational authors state it explicitly.
 b. Readers will have to infer this when an informational author never identifies it.
 c. Readers can identify it equally from neutral, balanced, or opinionated positions.
 d. Readers who have to analyze text to identify this can assume it is poorly written.

9. Which of the following is correct regarding basal readers for teaching reading?

 a. Basal readers involve a top-down approach.
 b. Reading sub-skills are taught systematically.
 c. Sequencing of teaching sub-skills is flexible.
 d. These have become rare in the twenty-first century.

10. Which of the following is true about children's writing skills?

 a. Writing skills and reading skills reciprocally improve one another.
 b. Writing skills are not apt to enhance learning as reading skills are.
 c. Writing skills come naturally to children and need not be taught.
 d. Writing skills meet any purpose or audience with the same style.

11. A class reads an essay about the benefits to youth of pet ownership. The author's position is very clear: She believes young people should be given the responsibility of taking care of pets. The author cites facts, research studies, and statistics to strengthen her position. This type of writing is called:

 a. Expository
 b. Narrative
 c. Persuasive
 d. Didactic

12. In the POWER strategy, which of the five writing steps in this model is one that students are notorious for most often neglecting?

   a. Organization
   b. Rewriting
   c. Planning
   d. Editing

13. In writing, _____ is the overall written expression of the writer's attitude, and _____ is the individual way in which the writer expresses the former.

   a. voice; tone
   b. tone; voice
   c. style; tone
   d. voice; style

14. Mr. Bennet's fourth-grade students are practicing digital literacy skills as part of a math unit on financial literacy. They will be completing two digital assignments during this unit. One assignment is to write a blog post on budgeting that will be published on the school website. Another assignment is to write an email to a friend describing something they are saving up to buy. Which topic would be most beneficial for Mr. Bennet to teach to assist students with successfully completing both of these assignments?

   a. Verifying online sources
   b. Selecting relevant search keywords
   c. Navigating nonlinear writing and hyperlinks in digital texts
   d. Adjusting formality of language based on audience

15. Which of these is most accurate about the research skill of formulating a research question?

   a. Students typically have no problem translating their source readings into writing.
   b. Teachers should begin by having students form questions on discussed concepts.
   c. Teachers should begin by having students form questions from assignment topics.
   d. Students may find certain graphic organizers helpful for this, but not mind-maps.

16. Which of these is true about children's development of spelling?

   a. Children must be able to read words to spell them.
   b. Children can spell without knowing letter patterns.
   c. Children usually can read words that they can spell.
   d. Children do not infer spelling of new spoken words.

17. Of the following, which sentence is correctly punctuated?

   a. "I told you that it would be ready next week; it will be ready next week."
   b. "I told you, that it would be ready next week it will be ready next week."
   c. "I told you that it would be ready next week, it will be ready next week."
   d. "I told you that it would be ready next week it will be ready next week."

18. Context clues are useful in:

   a. Predicting future action
   b. Understanding the meaning of words that are not familiar
   c. Understanding character motivation
   d. Reflecting on a text's theme

19. The phrase "Pretty as a picture" is *best* described as a:

   a. Metaphor
   b. Simile
   c. Duodenum's couple
   d. Figure of speech

20. Dr. Jenks is working with a group of students. They are about to read a science book about fossils. Before they begin, she writes the words *stromatolites, fossiliferous,* and *eocene* on the board. She explains the meaning of each word. These words are examples of:

   a. Academic words
   b. Alliteration
   c. Content-specific words
   d. Ionization

21. A teacher writes four sentences on the board and instructs his students to copy the sentences from the board into their notebooks. They must capitalize words with suffixes. Which sentence is correct?

   a. The PRINCE declared his undying love for the PRINCESS.
   b. Television is a form of MULTIMEDIA.
   c. This loud, loud noise is very DISPLEASING.
   d. The BOOKKEEPER examined every page of the rare play.

22. When students read informational text, they must be able to connect it with their existing knowledge and draw inferences from it to do which of the following?

   a. Comprehend the material enough to make conclusions, critical judgments, and interpretations
   b. Comprehend the material in the informational text thoroughly without doing anything further
   c. Comprehend the material and then make conclusions about it instead of any critical judgment
   d. Comprehend the material and produce their own interpretations of it rather than conclusions

23. Teachers must establish clear ground rules before initiating class or group discussions to ensure they actively listen and productively participate. Which of the following rules is *more* applicable to young children and students with behavior disorders than to all students equally?

   a. The rule of not participating in cross-talk
   b. The rule of not interrupting those talking
   c. The rule of not monopolizing discussions
   d. The rule of not hitting, kicking, biting, etc.

24. Among these components of speech delivery, which is most effective for establishing rapport and personal connection with audiences?

   a. Eye contact
   b. Vocal tones
   c. Articulation
   d. Movement

25. Which statement is most accurate regarding the whole language approach to literacy instruction in early childhood?

a. This approach does not emphasize giving children opportunities for independent reading.
b. This approach excludes activities that involve guided reading with small groups of children.
c. This approach believes children both learn to read by writing, and learn to write by reading.
d. This approach emphasizes early grammar, spelling, and other technical aspects are correct.

26. Of the following, which statement is true about instruction in the alphabetic principle?

a. Letter-sound relationships with the highest utility should be the earliest ones introduced.
b. The instruction of letter-sound correspondences should always be done in word context.
c. Letter-sound relationship practice times should only be assigned apart from other lessons.
d. Letter-sound relationship practice should focus on new relationships, not go over old ones.

27. Ms. Walters is planning her first-grade literacy block for the upcoming school year. Currently, she has guided reading time scheduled, where she plans to focus on individualized phonological awareness and phonics skills, decoding, and comprehension. Students will also reread some familiar texts for fluency practice and complete some phonological awareness and phonics-based word work stations. Ms. Walters also has time set aside for the whole class to read and analyze texts together to focus on comprehension skills, and they will write regularly in their journals. Which component of reading instruction should Ms. Walters add to best create a balanced literacy approach to instruction?

a. Phoneme blending
b. Vocabulary instruction
c. Identification of story elements
d. Using the alphabetic principle to spell words

28. Caret, carrot, to, two and too share something in common. They:

a. Are nouns
b. Are monosyllabic
c. Are homophones
d. Are dipthongs

29. Which of the following is NOT an example of problems or errors in student handwriting?

a. Faulty alignment
b. Incorrect spacing
c. Dangling participle
d. Writing is illegible

30. What description best represents how teachers promote language, literacy, and reading development by integrating it into their classroom instruction?

a. The teacher asks students during a science lesson to state hypotheses, observations, and conclusions orally.
b. The teacher asks students during a science lesson to write down hypotheses, observations, and conclusions.
c. The teacher models language and literacy participation by demonstrating writing apart from class discussion.
d. The teacher provides activities and games that promote exploring language and literacy in various groupings.

31. Which of these is a strategy most applicable to evaluating a young student's reading comprehension of narrative writing?
  a. Whether the student can retell a story that s/he has just read
  b. Whether the student can decode unfamiliar words in the story
  c. Whether the student can invent spellings for unfamiliar words
  d. Whether the student can identify and produce rhyming words

32. To help students understand abstract concepts in the print materials they read, which instructional aids that teachers provide can students *always* use three-dimensionally?
  a. Examples
  b. Manipulatives
  c. Graphic organizers
  d. Charts, tables, graphs

33. Syllable types include:
  a. Closed, open, silent *e*, vowel team, vowel-*r*, and consonant-*le*
  b. Closed, open, silent, double-vowel, *r*, and *le*
  c. Closed, midway, open, emphasized, prefixed, and suffixed
  d. Stressed, unstressed, and silent

34. Timothy, a first-grade student, writes a few sentences in his reading journal.

| February 8, |
| I played in the rane on Tuzday. I wore a cote to stay dry. I saw a grene frog by the car. |

Based on this writing sample, which skill should Timothy's teacher focus on first during small-group instruction?
  a. Spelling days of the week
  b. Consonant blends
  c. Long vowel spelling patterns
  d. R-controlled vowels.

35. Research has found which of the following outcomes occur for students via revision and rewriting?
  a. Students only correct their mechanical errors in revisions.
  b. Students often incorporate new ideas when they rewrite.
  c. Students retain their original writing goals during revision.
  d. Students' planning in prewriting is unaffected in rewriting.

36. Which of the following literary elements are MOST likely to be found in *both* fictional narratives *and* nonfictional informational text?
  a. The writing style of the author
  b. Labeled diagrams and photos
  c. Excitement and drama
  d. Themes and plots

Mathematics

37. When planning a unit on linear equations, a teacher would most likely include discussion on which of the following topics?

    a. Conjugating to remove irrational denominators
    b. Gradient of a straight line
    c. Order of operations
    d. Characteristics of the diagonals of various quadrilaterals

38. What is accurate regarding manipulative objects that can help young children learn math concepts?

    a. Teachers can find many math manipulatives for sale, and/or can make their own homemade ones.
    b. Teachers can only find helpful math manipulatives by buying those made by expert manufacturers.
    c. Teachers will save money and attain much greater learning benefits by hand-making manipulatives.
    d. Teachers should not waste money buying, or time making, these as children learn more from ideas.

39. In order to analyze the real estate market for two different zip codes within the city, a realtor examines the most recent 100 home sales in each zip code. She considered a house which sold within the first month of its listing to have a market time of one month; likewise, she considered a house to have a market time of two months if it sold after having been on the market for one month but by the end of the second month. Using this definition of market time, she determined the frequency of sales by number of months on the market. The results are displayed below.

Which of the following is a true statement for these data?

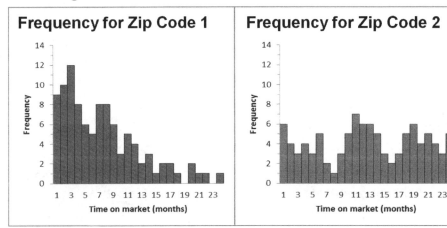

    a. The median time a house spends on the market in Zip Code 1 is five months less than Zip Code 2
    b. On average, a house spent seven months longer on the market in Zip Code 2 than in Zip Code 1.
    c. The mode time on the market is higher for Zip Code 1 than for Zip Code 2.
    d. The median time on the market is less than the mean time on the market for Zip Code 1.

40. Of the following, which is accurate regarding the relationship of problem-solving skills to math?

    a. Children are not interested in solving everyday problems; adults must give incentives.
    b. Children learn mathematical thinking; other things promote language and social skills.
    c. Children learn through solving problems that there can be multiple possible solutions.
    d. Children should not propose problems or ask questions about them; the adults should.

41. A circular bracelet contains 5 charms, A, B, C, D, and E, attached at specific points around the bracelet, with the clasp located between charms A and B. The bracelet is unclasped and stretched out into a straight line. On the resulting linear bracelet, charm C is between charms A and B, charm D is between charms A and C, and charm E is between charms C and D. Which of these statements is (are) necessarily true?

    I. The distance between charms B and E is greater than the distance between charms A and D.
    II. Charm E is between charms B and D.
    III. The distance between charms D and E is less than the distance of bracelet between charms A and C.

    a. I, II, and III
    b. II and III
    c. II only
    d. None of these must be true.

42. Ms. Chen is instructing her students on divisibility rules. Which of the following rules can be used to determine if a number is divisible by 6?

    a. The last digit of the number is divisible by 2 or 3.
    b. The number ends in 6.
    c. The number is divisible by 2 and 3.
    d. The last two digits of the number are divisible by 6.

43. Of the following, which is/are NOT an example(s) of math manipulatives?

    a. Tangrams for shape recognition
    b. Large magnetic number boards
    c. Printed mathematical formulas
    d. Play money, toy cash registers

44. Which of the following is true regarding children's development of number sense?

    a. Children must learn all number names before they learn to count.
    b. Children learn to count before learning all the names of numbers.
    c. Children's number sense is equal to, and a synonym for, counting.
    d. Children's number sense is that numbers only describe quantities.

45. A gift box has a length of 14 inches, a height of 8 inches, and a width of 6 inches. How many square inches of wrapping paper are needed to wrap the box?

    a. 56
    b. 244
    c. 488
    d. 672

46. Eli rolls a die and tosses a coin. What is the probability he gets a prime number or tails?

   a. $\dfrac{1}{4}$

   b. $\dfrac{1}{3}$

   c. $\dfrac{1}{2}$

   d. $\dfrac{3}{4}$

47. What can adults do to help young children develop their number sense and numeracy skills?

   a. Counting real objects in the environment is very useful.
   b. Sorting by color, shape, or size is irrelevant to numbers.
   c. Sorting by difference is better than sorting by similarity.
   d. Sorting by similarity is better than sorting by difference.

48. Regarding problem-solving skills and how they apply to mathematics, which of the following is true?

   a. In math, there is always only one possible right answer to a given question.
   b. Students must learn the concept that multiple solutions to a problem exist.
   c. Problem-solving skills are important for only certain parts of mathematics.
   d. Problem-solving skills can be learned equally well with or without practice.

49. Which statement is true regarding children's basic understanding of patterns and relationships?

   a. This understanding is unrelated to children's understanding of repetition.
   b. Having this is unlikely to inform children in any understanding of rhythm.
   c. Children can understand grouping things into categories if they have this.
   d. Children need different knowledge for ordering things by size or degree.

50. What is the distance on a coordinate plane from (−8, 6) to (4, 3)?

   a. $\sqrt{139}$
   b. $\sqrt{147}$
   c. $\sqrt{153}$
   d. $\sqrt{161}$

51. $A = \{9, 4, -3, 8, 6, 0\}$ and $B = \{-4, 2, 8, 9, 0\}$. What is $A \cup B$?

   a. $\{9, 8, 0\}$
   b. $\{9, 4, -3, 8, 6, 0, -4, 2\}$
   c. $\emptyset$
   d. $\{9, 8, 0, 2, 4\}$

52. On a floor plan drawn at a scale of 1:100, the area of a rectangular room is 30 cm². What is the actual area of the room?

   a. $30,000 \text{ cm}^2$
   b. $3,000 \text{ cm}^2$
   c. $3,000 \text{ m}^2$
   d. 30 m^2

53. Which of the following activities is most focused on children's *identifying* patterns?
   a. Stringing beads with different colors in a certain order to make a necklace design
   b. Counting the number of blue dots before a green dot appears in a printed fabric
   c. Arranging alternating pieces of different sizes and gluing them to paper or board
   d. Hopping two times on one foot, then the other; then three times each; four; etc.

54. Which is most accurate regarding what constitutes number sense in young children?
   a. Number sense encompasses understanding of all the ways that we apply numbers.
   b. Number sense is understanding that we use numbers to communicate information.
   c. Number sense is understanding that we use numbers for manipulating information.
   d. Number sense is knowing we use numbers to describe quantities and relationships.

55. Which of the following expressions is equivalent to $-3x(x-2)^2$?
   a. $-3x^3 + 6x^2 - 12x$
   b. $-3x^3 - 12x^2 + 12x$
   c. $-3x^2 + 6x$
   d. $-3x^3 + 12x^2 - 12x$

56. McKenzie shades $\frac{1}{5}$ of a piece of paper. Then, she shades an additional area $\frac{1}{5}$ the size of what she just shaded. Next, she shades another area $\frac{1}{5}$ as large as the previous one. As she continues the process to infinity, what is the limit of the shaded fraction of the paper?
   a. $\frac{1}{5}$
   b. $\frac{1}{4}$
   c. $\frac{1}{3}$
   d. $\frac{1}{2}$

57. Which of the following represents the net of a triangular prism?

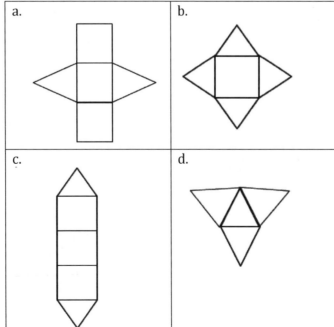

58. Andrew rolls a die. What is the probability he gets a 4 or an even number?

 a. $\dfrac{1}{4}$

 b. $\dfrac{1}{2}$

 c. $\dfrac{2}{3}$

 d. $\dfrac{3}{4}$

59. Which of the following learning goals is most appropriate for a second-grade unit on personal financial literacy?

 a. The students will be able to calculate how money saved can accumulate into a larger amount over time.
 b. The students will be able to balance a simple budget.
 c. The students will be able to identify the costs and benefits of planned and unplanned spending decisions.
 d. The students will be able to define money earned as income.

60. Which of the following options represents equivalency between different representations of rational numbers?

 a. $16 \div (6-4)^2 = 64$
 b. $8 - 2(7-4) = 18$
 c. $2^3 \div 2 - 2(2) = 0$
 d. $2 + 3(2^2) = 20$

61. Claus has $20 to spend at the local fun fair. The entrance fee is $2.50 and tickets for the booths are $2 each. Which of the following inequalities represents the number of tickets Claus can afford with his $20?

 a. $2.50x + 2x \le 20$
 b. $2.50 + 2x \le 20$
 c. $2x \le 20 + 2.50$
 d. $2.50 + 2x \ge 20x$

62. A teacher is assessing the students' understanding of the appropriate units for length, area, and volume. Which of the following only lists units of area?

 a. in^2, mm^2, ft^2
 b. yd, yd^2, yd^3
 c. mm, cm, m
 d. m^2, s^2, km^2

63. Ms. Elliott asks her students, "Do you prefer chocolate or vanilla ice cream?" If the probability of her students preferring chocolate ice cream is 0.6, what is the probability of her students preferring vanilla ice cream?

 a. 0.6
 b. 0.4
 c. 0.3
 d. 0.5

14

64. While teaching the concept of addition, a first-grade teacher gives each student two dice to use as manipulatives. Which of the following types of representation is this teacher using to communicate this concept?

 a. Concrete
 b. Verbal
 c. Graphic
 d. Pictorial

65. Which of these adult behaviors is most conducive to developing children's reasoning skills?

 a. When adults analyze children's thought processes and then explain them to the children
 b. When adults ask children questions, allow them time to think, and listen to their answers
 c. When adults tell children why something exists/is a certain way and discuss it with them
 d. When adults classify objects or concepts into groups to demonstrate logic to the children

66. The variables *x* and *y* are in a linear relationship. The table below shows a few sample values. Which of the following graphs correctly represents the linear equation relating *x* and *y*?

x	y
−2	−11
−1	−8
0	−5
1	−2
2	1

a.

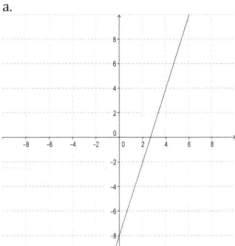

b.

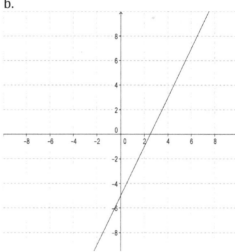

c.

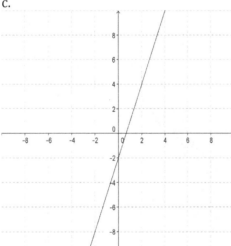

d.

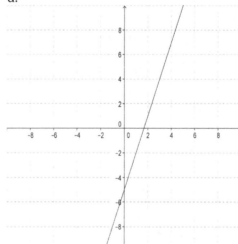

Science

67. Among these everyday activities of young children, which most helps them develop concepts of 1:1 correspondence?

    a. Seeing how many coins are in a piggy bank or children are in their group
    b. Distributing one item to each child in the group or fitting pegs into holes
    c. Dividing up objects into piles by their types or by having the same shape
    d. Transferring sand/rice/water among various container shapes and sizes

68. In the scientific method, which of the following steps should come first?

    a. Formulating a hypothesis
    b. Asking a research question
    c. Conducting an experiment
    d. Reporting proof or disproof

69. In the scientific process, which skill do children employ most when they see patterns and meaning in the results of experiments they make?

    a. Measurement
    b. Classification
    c. Inferences
    d. Prediction

70. Limestone is one example of which subtype of sedimentary rock?

    a. Clastic
    b. Organic
    c. Chemical
    d. Pegmatite

71. When young children build structures from blocks and then knock them down or take them apart, which of these science concepts are they learning?

    a. Concepts of shape
    b. Concepts of weight
    c. Part-whole relations
    d. Temporal sequences

72. A pulley lifts a 10 kg object 10 m into the air in 5 minutes. Using this information, you can calculate:

    a. mechanical advantage
    b. efficiency
    c. energy conservation
    d. power

73. Two companion models, gradualism and punctuated equilibrium, dominate evolutionary theory. Which of the following statements is MOST consistent with the theory of punctuated equilibrium?

    a. Fossils show changes over large periods of time.
    b. Fossils showing intermediate characteristics may not necessarily be found.
    c. Speciation occurs gradually.
    d. Evolution is a slow, steady process.

74. Which of the following is true?

    a. Materials whose atoms have strongly bound electrons conduct.
    b. Materials whose atoms have loose electrons insulate electricity.
    c. Materials with free electrons block the conduction of electricity.
    d. Materials whose atoms feature tightly bound electrons insulate.

75. When light passes between different transparent media, its speed is changed by the change in medium and it is refracted, as when a straw in a glass of water seems to break or bend at the waterline. The amount that a medium slows down the speed of light is the:

    a. Normal line
    b. Wavelength
    c. Index of refraction
    d. Angle of refraction

76. Which of the following is true about how light is absorbed?

    a. The sky is blue because the atmosphere reflects only blue wavelengths.
    b. The sky is blue because the atmosphere absorbs only blue wavelengths.
    c. Glass is transparent to all of the frequencies of light within the spectrum.
    d. Wood, metal, and other opaque materials reflect all wavelengths of light.

77. How are animals of the Mollusca phylum able to respire?

    a. Through gills
    b. Through a trachea
    c. Through lungs
    d. Through muscle contraction

78. Among the states of matter, water vapor is classified as:

    a. A gas.
    b. A solid.
    c. A liquid.
    d. A plasma.

79. Which states of matter are not fluids?

    a. Solids
    b. Plasma
    c. Liquids
    d. Gases

80. What is the purpose of conducting an experiment?

    a. to test a hypothesis
    b. to collect data
    c. to identify a control state
    d. to choose variables

81. In insects whose life cycles include an incomplete metamorphosis, which stage of the metamorphosis does not take place?

a. The egg
b. The larva
c. The imago
d. The pupa

82. One complete revolution of the Earth around the Sun equals:

a. One day.
b. One year.
c. One month.
d. One century.

83. Of the following ecological relationships, which ones benefit both organisms involved?

a. Commensalistic relationships
b. Mutualistic relationships
c. Parasitic relationships
d. None of these does

Social Studies

84. Which of the following behaviors typically develops earliest in babies/toddlers/young children?

a. Coordinating their peer-play behaviors
b. Sharing toy/object activities with peers
c. Prosocial, helping, and caring behaviors
d. Creating "make-believe" play scenarios

85. According to psychologist Diana Baumrind, which of the parenting styles she identified is the ideal?

a. Authoritarian
b. Authoritative
c. Uninvolved
d. Permissive

86. What accurately reflects acculturation vs. assimilation?

a. Ethnic groups' uniting to form a new culture is acculturation.
b. A dominant culture's absorbing other cultures is assimilation.
c. Assimilation is when cultures adopt traits from other cultures.
d. When two or more cultures virtually fuse, this is assimilation.

87. Which of the following is/are accurate about individualistic vs. collectivist orientations of some world cultures?

a. Latin American and African cultures are more often individualistic.
b. Individualism is less common in Canadian and Australian cultures.
c. Native American and Asian cultures are typically more collectivist.
d. European and North American cultures tend to be more collectivist.

88. Which part of a hurricane features the strongest winds and greatest rainfall?

   a. Eye wall
   b. Front
   c. Eye
   d. Outward spiral

89. Which of the following correctly shows the chronological progress in EC development of five levels of self-awareness?

   a. Identification, self-consciousness, differentiation, situation, permanence
   b. Situation, differentiation, self-consciousness, permanence, identification
   c. Self-consciousness, identification, differentiation, permanence, situation
   d. Differentiation, situation, identification, permanence, self-consciousness

90. What is accurate regarding popular conflict resolution approaches for young children?

   a. EC conflict mediation steps are similar to the steps of adult conflict mediation.
   b. Adults should listen to emotions children express but should not say anything.
   c. Adults should gather information about a conflict but not talk directly about it.
   d. Suggesting possible conflict solutions should be done by an adult, not children.

91. According to family systems theory, which statement is accurate regarding family boundaries?

   a. Disengaged families have more restricted/closed boundaries.
   b. Enmeshed families place a greater value upon independence.
   c. Disengaged families are more open to considering new input.
   d. Enmeshed families have looser and more flexible boundaries.

92. On a geographical map, which of the following requires using a ratio to interpret?

   a. The key or legend
   b. The compass rose
   c. The scale of miles
   d. The lines in a grid

93. Among the following, which is correct regarding some essential geography concepts?

   a. An example of absolute location is urban vs. rural land prices.
   b. Relative location equals the latitude and longitude of a place.
   c. Product and land prices are affected by geographical distance.
   d. Achievability relates to surface conditions and never changes.

94. Of the four parenting styles identified by psychologists, which one is found most likely to result in children who have problems with authority figures, poor school performance, and poor self-regulation?

   a. Authoritarian
   b. Permissive
   c. Authoritative
   d. Uninvolved

95. Of the following, what is most accurate about how cultural expression influences human behavior?

    a. African-American culture has historically developed a strong oral tradition.
    b. Latin American culture has not influenced North American music or dance.
    c. Recent Asian immigrants immediately adopt American family organization.
    d. European-American policy has not affected Native American tribal culture.

96. People are typically made aware of political, facts, and values through family, friends, society, and:

    a. Media
    b. Census takers
    c. History
    d. Gun ownership

97. In a popular set of six conflict-mediation/resolution steps for young children, the first step is to approach the conflict calmly, interrupting any hurtful behaviors; the second step is to acknowledge the children's feelings. Of the subsequent four steps, which comes first?

    a. Gather enough information about the conflict.
    b. Elicit potential solutions; help children pick one.
    c. Reiterate/state over again what the problem is.
    d. Provide the children with support as is needed.

98. A typically developing child is shown a TV with live video of herself, and also shown adult researchers who are imitating the child's behaviors. The child can tell the difference between the video and the imitators. This child is most likely:

    a. A newborn
    b. Two years old
    c. Four to seven months
    d. Four to six months

99. The interdependence of rural and urban regions on one another for their materials and products is an example of which of the following geographical concepts?

    a. Interaction
    b. Area Differentiation
    c. Both (A) and (D)
    d. Spatial Interrelatedness

100. What is a correct reason for laws and rules that can be used to help young children understand important concepts of civics?

    a. Laws and rules punish rather than identify unacceptable citizen behaviors.
    b. Laws and rules interfere with the ability of citizens to have responsibilities.
    c. Laws and rules make society and life more predictable, orderly, and secure.
    d. Laws and rules grant greater powers to persons with positions of authority.

Arts

101. Which of the following artistic elements would be found only in sculpture or decorative arts?

    a. Line
    b. Form
    c. Proportion
    d. Balance

102. If a class curriculum involves a unit on space travel, which of these would thematically integrate an art activity for the students?

    a. Painting portraits of their classmates
    b. Constructing models of rocket ships
    c. Exploring materials all in one color
    d. Using art to express their feelings

103. Visual literacy can best be described as the

    a. ability to communicate through images and comprehend the messages contained in images.
    b. ability to construct three-dimensional images mentally.
    c. seamless incorporation of literary text into works of art.
    d. incorporation of art into literary texts, such as illumination.

104. An EC teacher has children lie down on butcher paper in whatever body positions they choose and outlines their body shapes with a marker. Then the teacher has the children enhance and personalize these outlines by drawing different kinds of lines with various tools. What is correct about this activity?

    a. The children will learn how line is used in visual art and about drawing different kinds of lines.
    b. The children will not learn as much from this activity as from shapes that are not their own.
    c. The children will learn more about how shape is used in art than about how lines are used.
    d. The children will learn kinesthetic concepts from posing their bodies but not anything about art.

105. What is the difference between 3/4 time and 6/8 time, by definition?

    a. There is no difference.
    b. 3/4 time uses three beats per measure, while 6/8 time uses six beats per measure.
    c. In 3/4 time the quarter note acts as the one beat unit, while in 6/8 time the eighth note acts as the one beat unit.
    d. 3/4 time uses a quicker tempo.

106. The purpose of an artist portfolio is most often to

    a. demonstrate an artist's capabilities.
    b. communicate past work history and education.
    c. teach an artist's students.
    d. include all artwork for copyright purposes.

107. Which of the following composers is most strongly associated with the Romantic Period?

  a. Johann Sebastian Bach
  b. Maurice Ravel
  c. Aaron Copeland
  d. Johannes Brahms

108. Which of the following is not true of careers in the art industry?

  a. The majority of artists are self-employed.
  b. Few artists bother earning postsecondary degrees or certificates.
  c. Competition is keen for salaried jobs in the art industry.
  d. Annual earnings for artists vary widely.

109. In order to for a pigment to reach the desired consistency for fluid painting, with which of the following should it not be combined?

  a. Turpentine
  b. Fresco
  c. A tempera
  d. An oil medium

110. When we perceive a painting, song, dance, or play as cohesive, with all elements belonging together and combining to create a completely realized whole whereby the artist effectively communicates the mood, atmosphere, feeling, and story, this reflects the organizing principle of:

  a. Repetition
  b. Contrast
  c. Balance
  d. Unity

Health and Physical Education

111. Which parts of the human musculoskeletal system are NOT types of connective tissue?

  a. Ligaments
  b. Tendons
  c. Cartilage
  d. Joints

112. Which of these infant reflexes normally disappears at the latest ages?

  a. Babinski reflex
  b. Stepping reflex
  c. Grasping reflex
  d. The tonic reflex

113. For adults to protect children from environmental health risk, which of these is true?

  a. House dust that accumulates in homes is not considered a health risk.
  b. Parents should use only cold water to prepare formula to feed babies.
  c. The presence of carbon monoxide gas indoors is normal and harmless.
  d. Infants and young children need sunlight, so it is safe to expose them.

114. Regarding physical, emotional, and social factors that influence personal physical health, which of the following is true?

  a. Anxiety and depression cause sleep and diet problems but not cardiovascular troubles.
  b. Stress and family dysfunction cause emotional problems, not physical illness.
  c. Air pollution can aggravate asthma but is not actually found to cause asthma.
  d. People can overeat and be overweight, and yet still suffer from malnutrition.

115. Which of the following are targeted by the 2009 American Recovery and Reinvestment Act as the primary preventable causes of disability and death?

  a. Obesity and tobacco use
  b. Alcohol and tobacco use
  c. Obesity and alcohol use
  d. Alcohol and drug abuse

116. Of the following motor skills, which do babies or toddlers typically develop the latest?

  a. Play "pattycake"
  b. Pull up to stand
  c. Jumping in place
  d. The pincer grasp

117. According to research studies, what is true about the impact of physical activity (PA) on health risks?

  a. PA lowers heart disease, stroke, diabetes, and colon and breast cancer risks.
  b. PA reduces risks of heart disease and stroke but not of diabetes or any cancer.
  c. PA reduces risks of all these diseases, but amounts of PA needed for each disease vary greatly.
  d. PA in adequate amounts improves overall well-being but does not lower disease risks.

118. Which of the following is MOST appropriate concerning extracurricular activities for student health needs?

  a. A student should expect to feel overextended when participating in activities.
  b. A student should discontinue an activity if he or she cannot keep up with all things.
  c. A student should join only those activities that he or she already knows how to do.
  d. A student should always try new things, regardless of time constraints.

119. Which of these is most closely linked with symptoms resembling those of ADHD in children?

  a. Skipping breakfast
  b. Often missing meals
  c. Deficiencies in iron
  d. Protein deficiencies

120. Which of the following best sums up the theory of deliberate practice?

  a. Practice makes perfect
  b. Natural athletes require little practice
  c. Long bouts of practice are most effective
  d. Reflection is a necessary aspect of practice

Answer Key and Explanations #1

Language Arts

1. B: The One-Word stage typically begins when children are about one year old. Their utterances consist of single words, some of which are real words and some invented words, also known as idiomorphs. For example, a child may consistently use the idiomorphs "bankie" to mean his or her special security blanket. In the Cooing stage (A), infants around six weeks and older naturally begin to make vowel-like sounds as they experiment with their oral skills. In the Telegraphic stage (C), toddlers produce utterances of several words, but without any connecting function words like articles (e.g., "the" or "those"), prepositions (e.g., "on," "in," "to"); plural or possessive endings ("s") or other morphemes. For example, they may say "Daddy hat" to mean "Daddy's hat." In the Babbling stage (D), infants about 4–6 months and older begin to produce consonant-vowel combinations that they repeat, like "ba-ba-ba." By about 8–10 months old, infant babbling develops the rhythms and intonations, without the actual words, of adult speech.

2. B: Norm-referenced tests compare a student's scores to the scores of a sample of students that are representative of the population for the same age, developmental level, or grade. They show how a student's performance compares to the average and whether that student is achieving significantly above or below the norm. Therefore, to tell parents if their children perform above average and may be gifted or below average and may have developmental disabilities, educators would administer norm-referenced tests. Criterion-referenced tests compare a student's scores to a performance standard for the student's age, developmental level, or grade, which has been pre-determined by educational experts. They show how a student's performance compares to established standards. To tell parents if their children have mastered all areas of development or whether and how children's mastery levels have changed over time, educators would administer criterion-referenced tests.

3. D: Normally developing preschoolers typically develop print awareness skills that include all of these: reciting the alphabet; recognizing both printed letters and printed words; and using print as a vehicle for communication.

4. D: Phonemes are the smallest units of sound in words. In this activity, students are replacing one phoneme with another, which is known as phoneme substitution. Alliteration refers to a series of words in which most words begin with the same sound. Segmenting refers to breaking a word down into its individual sounds, or phonemes. Onset and rime blending involve blending the beginning sound of a word with the rest of the word.

5. A: Letter–sound correspondence. Letter–sound correspondence relies on the relationship between a spoken sound or group of sounds and the letters conventionally used in English to write them.

6. D: Rate, accuracy, and prosody. Fluent readers are able to read smoothly and comfortably at a steady pace (rate). The more quickly a child reads, the greater the chance of leaving out a word or substituting one word for another (for example, *sink* instead of *shrink*). Fluent readers are able to maintain accuracy without sacrificing rate. Fluent readers also stress important words in a text, group words into rhythmic phrases, and read with intonation (prosody).

7. A: Students need to know why and how to use text features to inform their reading. Reading headings above sections within chapters (A) help students determine the main subject matter of

25

each section. Reading the glossary for a chapter (B) gives students definitions of terms used in the chapter. Reading the index in a text (C) is a way to locate page numbers of references to subjects or authors in the text. Whether they will be reading the entire section or not, students need not read through the whole thing (D) only to determine its subject matter when its heading will typically indicate this. Headings inform students of topics in advance if they will be reading the section; if they are doing research or choosing what to read, headings can help them decide.

8. B: Authors of informational texts do explicitly state their point of view and/or purpose sometimes, but NOT always (a); many authors do not overtly identify it, so readers must infer it (b), which is easier when the author's position is more opinionated, but harder when it is neutral or balanced (c)—or when the text itself is difficult. Therefore, readers have to analyze some text to identify author point of view or purpose, which they should NOT assume indicates poor writing (d).

9. B: The basal reader approach is bottom-up in nature, not top-down (A); i.e., sub-skills for reading are taught from smaller to larger parts and parts to whole. Students are aided in transitions from the part to the whole through instruction in a systematic (B) sequence that is followed rigidly, and is not flexible (C). While fewer publishers have issued basal reading series in the twenty-first century than in the twentieth, the basal reader approach to teaching reading is still the most common one in America: approximately 75% to 85% of classrooms in grades K–8 still use basal readers, so they are not at all rare (D). Other than the number of publishers offering them, the main difference is that previous basal reading series before/during the twentieth century emphasized vocabulary control and skill acquisition at the expense of comprehension and pleasure; whereas twenty-first-century basal readers enhance student motivation to read more with multiple versions of stories, book excerpts enabling selection sharing, and other sources of greater variety.

10. A: Literacy research shows that reading and writing development have mutual benefits: improving one improves the other, and vice versa. Researchers find that children's capacity to learn is increased by increases in *both* reading and writing skills (B). Educational researchers have also found that to write well, children must have instruction; it is not a skill set that comes naturally to them (C). It is not true that having good writing skills enables the writer to meet any purpose or audience using the same single writing style (D): a part of learning writing skills is learning the ability to vary one's style and write in different genres to suit different purposes (e.g., to persuade, to inform, to amuse, or to express ideas and feelings) and different intended audiences (e.g., using different language, tone, and references that are relevant to and appeal to different readers).

11. C: Persuasive. The author is hoping to persuade or convince readers to either request a pet and/or the primary care of their pet by providing them with facts as well as by using rhetorical devices such as dispelling opposing arguments.

12. C: The POWER strategy, one popular writing instruction model, features five steps. Planning, the first step, is one many students tend to neglect: they simply plunge in and start writing without any pre-writing work. Planning includes choosing a topic: teachers help students complete a Yes/No checklist about whether a good topic was chosen, and also help them research and read about the topic, consider information readers would want, and write down all topic-related ideas. In Organization (A), the second step, teachers help students see if they grouped related ideas, chose the best ones for the composition, and logically numbered/ordered them. The third step is writing, including all ideas in full sentences and getting help as needed from texts, teachers, or classmates. The fourth step, Editing (D), includes reading the first draft, marking parts s/he likes and those s/he might change, and reading it to a classmate to hear feedback. The fifth step, rewriting (B), involves making needed changes, correcting mechanics, and the final draft.

13. B: Tone is the way in which the writer writes overall to express his or her attitude. Voice is who the reader hears speaking in the writing, the individual way the writer uses to express his or her tone—not vice versa. Style is the effect a writer creates through language, mechanics, and attitude or the sound (formal or informal) or impressions (seriousness, levity, grace, fluency) of the writing.

14. D: Although all of the skills listed are part of digital literacy, the main focus of this assignment is to create writing on the same topic for two very different audiences. Students will therefore need to know how to adjust the formality of their writing so that it is appropriate for each audience. A post on the school website, which will be seen by numerous community members, should use a more formal tone than an email to a friend. Therefore, choice D is the most relevant skill for this particular assignment.

15. C: Many students lack understanding of connecting reading to writing on research topics (a). Teachers can help them learn to formulate research questions as the first writing step through early activities like converting assignment topics into core questions and related subordinate questions (c) to approach sources. Once students have enough practice, in later years, teachers can lead class discussions of concepts and have students formulate research questions about these (b). One graphic organizer students often find helps organize ideas and arguments are mind maps (d), with the question central, and pro and con arguments and supporting references as branches.

16. C: Children do not necessarily have to be able to read words in order to spell them (A). In fact, once children learn how to spell certain words, they can usually then read them (C) in text. With experience, children notice basic patterns in letter combinations that form syllables, roots that many related words share in common, common word endings (e.g., *-tion, -ate*, etc.), commonly used prefixes and suffixes, etc. Knowledge of these patterns, together with the basic spelling principles and rules of their language, are prerequisites to learning to spell; hence (B) is incorrect. Once they have learned these prerequisite patterns, principles, and rules, children typically *do* infer the correct spellings of many new words when they hear them spoken (D).

17. A: This version is correctly punctuated because it is a compound-complex sentence, consisting of two independent clauses and a dependent/subordinate (relative) clause. Independent clauses should be separated by a semicolon. In (B) and (D), the two independent clauses have no punctuation separating them, creating a run-on sentence; additionally, (B) has an incorrect comma between the first independent clause and the subordinating conjunction "that," which introduces the relative clause. (If "that" were omitted, it would be correct with or without the comma.) Version (C) incorrectly separates the independent clauses with a comma instead of a semicolon.

18. B: Understanding the meaning of words that are not familiar. Context clues offer insight into the probable meaning of unfamiliar words.

19. B: "Pretty as a picture" is a simile (comparison of two unlike things using the words *like* or *as*).

20. C: Because these words are specific to paleontology, it's unlikely the students know their meanings. Without understanding what these words mean, the students would not be able to understand the content of the passage they were about to read.

21. C: The word *displeasing* contains the root *please* and has both a prefix and a suffix. The *-ing* acts as the suffix in displeasing, therefore it is correctly capitalized.

22. A: Students must be able to connect informational text they read with their existing knowledge and draw inferences from it in order to not only comprehend the material alone (b), but also to make conclusions AND critical judgments about it (c), as well as their own interpretations of it (d).

23. D: Good ground rules for teachers to establish before initiating class or group discussions include no cross-talk (a), no interrupting others (b), and no monopolizing the discussion (c), all of which may apply equally to all students. However, the rule prohibiting hitting, kicking, biting (d) or similar aggressive physical contact is more applicable to young children and students with behavior disorders, as these behaviors are not common among all other students.

24. A: Speakers can establish rapport and personal connection with audiences by making eye contact with all listeners. They can express enthusiasm, emphasize important points, and maintain audience attention by varying their vocal tones (b). They ensure better hearing and comprehension by more listeners by using clear articulation (c). They can clarify and/or emphasize messages and promote audience perceptions of their credibility through body movement (d) and gestures as well as the other components named.

25. C: The whole language approach to early childhood literacy instruction does espouse the belief that learning reading and writing are each reciprocally active in helping children to learn the other. It does emphasize giving children many opportunities to read independently (A). It also includes activities involving guided reading with small groups of children (B). This approach does not emphasize children's early correctness with grammar, spelling, or other technical aspects of language (D), as children needing explicit instruction in decoding skills and strategies would have problems with them.

26. A: While there is no consensus among experts as to any universal sequence of instruction for teaching the alphabetic principle through phonics instruction, they do agree that, to enable children to start reading words as soon as possible, the highest-utility relationships should be introduced earliest. For example, the letters *m*, *a*, *p*, *t*, and *s* are all used frequently, whereas the *x* in *box*, the sound of *ey* in *they*, and the letter *a* when pronounced as it is in *want* have lower-utility letter-sound correspondences. Important considerations for the alphabetic principle are to teach letter-sound correspondences in isolation, not in word contexts (B); to teach them explicitly; to give students opportunities to practice letter-sound relationships within their other daily lessons, not only separately (C); and to include cumulative reviews of relationships taught earlier along with new ones in practice opportunities (D).

27. B: The five major components of balanced literacy instruction are phonological awareness, phonics, fluency, comprehension, and vocabulary. Ms. Walters' plan does not currently include any specialized vocabulary instruction. Vocabulary knowledge can assist with decoding, as students can use knowledge of the words and the cueing systems to figure out unknown words. It can also assist with comprehension, as vocabulary words often hold meaning in the texts. Additionally, it can assist with fluency by enabling readers to quickly and automatically recognize complex words. Phoneme blending is part of phonological awareness, identification of story elements is part of comprehension, and using the alphabetic principle to spell words is part of phonics.

28. C: Are homophones. Homophones are words that are pronounced the same but differ in meaning. For example, a bride wears a 2 caret ring, but a horse eats a carrot. These words are not all nouns or monosyllabic, and none of them are dipthongs. Dipthongs (D) are a single-syllable sound made up by combining two vowels, such as in the words *weird*, *applause*, and *boy*.

29. C: A dangling participle is an example of an error in grammar rather than in handwriting. (For example, the sentence "While growing up, my parents taught me...." has a dangling participle or misplaced modifier: the modifier refers to the object [me], not the subject [my parents].) Examples of student errors in handwriting include incorrect or poor alignment (A) of letters, words, and/or lines; incorrect spacing (B) between letters and/or words; and writing illegibly (D), i.e., readers cannot decipher what letters/words were intended by the writer.

30. D: Literacy experts describe how teachers can integrate language, literacy, and reading development into classroom instruction as including asking students during science lessons to state their hypotheses, observations, and conclusions BOTH orally (a) AND in writing (b); modeling language and literacy participation by demonstrating writing, e.g., by writing student comments on the board during class discussions (c); and providing activities and games that promote exploring language and literacy independently, one-to-one, and in peer groups (d).

31. A: Narrative writing is storytelling, as opposed to expository or informational writing. Ability to retell the story is a key strategy for assessing a student's reading comprehension. Decoding new words (B), inventing original spellings for new words (C), and identifying and producing rhymes (D) are all abilities whereby teachers can assess student skills for decoding printed words, but not their comprehension of printed text.

32. B: Manipulatives are three-dimensional concrete objects that students can not only look at but also touch, move, dismantle and reassemble (in some cases), rearrange, etc —i.e., manipulate, as the name indicates. Examples may be three-dimensional objects, demonstrations, or (more often) verbal descriptions given orally, printed, or written. Graphic organizers are diagrams (e.g., Venn diagrams), charts, timelines, concept maps, word webs, etc. which are two-dimensional, visual, graphic materials. Charts, tables, and graphs, though less pictorial and conceptual and more linear and numerical than graphic organizers, are also two-dimensional in print, online, or on screen.

33. A: Closed, open, silent *e*, vowel team, vowel-*r*, and consonant-*le*. A closed syllable ends with a consonant, such as *cat*. Open syllables end with a vowel, such as *he*. Vowel team syllables contain two vowels working together, such as *main*. Vowel-*r* syllables such as *er* and *or* frequently occur as suffixes. Consonant-*le* syllables also typically occur as suffixes, such as *battle* or *terrible*.

34. C: Timothy made several mistakes when spelling long vowel sounds, using the CVCe spelling pattern for words that have two vowels in the middle. Because he made multiple errors with this spelling pattern and it can be applied to many other common words, it would be beneficial for the teacher to focus on this skill first. Although Timothy spelled *Tuesday* incorrectly, it is a more complex word that will likely take time and repetition to learn. He also will not be able to generalize that skill to spell many other words. He spelled the words with r-controlled vowels, *wore* and *car*, correctly.

35. B: Researchers have found that the writing processes both form a hierarchy and are observably recursive in nature. Moreover, they find that when students continually revise their writing, they are able to consider new ideas and to incorporate these ideas into their work. Thus, they do not merely correct mechanical errors when revising (A), they also add to the content and quality of their writing. Furthermore, research shows that writers, including students, not only revise their actual writing; during rewrites, they also reconsider their original writing goals rather than always retaining them (C), and they revisit their prewriting plans rather than leaving these unaffected in rewriting (D).

36. A: In both the fictional narrative genre and the nonfictional informational genre, the author will demonstrate some individual writing style; even very factual and objective expositional writing will reveal some personal stylistic characteristics. Labeled diagrams and photos are more likely to be found in informational nonfiction. The majority of books with excitement and drama are fictional narratives (some informational nonfiction books are presented in narrative form and include excitement, especially in children's literature, but these are the minority). Themes and plots are also literary elements associated with fictional narrative.

Mathematics

37. B: The gradient of a straight line refers to the slope of the line. This concept is vital to understanding linear equations.

38. A: It is possible for teachers to use effective manipulative objects to instruct young children in early math concepts by purchasing, constructing, and finding them. Geometric shapes, linking cubes, magnetized numbers and boards; weights and scales; math games and blocks; tangrams; color tiles; flash cards; play money and working toy cash registers, etc., can be bought from stores, catalogs, and online. Teachers can also construct useful math manipulatives from everyday materials, and they can use found objects without further assembly, like pebbles, seashells, buttons, bottle caps, keys, cardboard tubes, coffee stirrers, etc. It is not true that either buying (B) or making (C) manipulatives is superior; teachers can do one, the other, or both depending on budgets, time, availability, and preference. Young children learn best when ideas are embodied in concrete physical objects they can look at, touch, and handle, rather than when ideas are presented to them abstractly (D).

39. D: Since there are 100 homes' market times represented in each set, the median time a home spends on the market is between the 50th and 51st data point in each set. The 50th and 51st data points for Zip Code 1 are six months and seven months, respectively, so the median time a house in Zip Code 1 spends on the market is between six and seven months (6.5 months), which by the realtor's definition of market time is a seven-month market time. The 50th and 51st data points for Zip Code 2 are both thirteen months, so the median time a house in Zip Code 2 spends on the market is thirteen months.

To find the mean market time for 100 houses, find the sum of the market times and divide by 100. If the frequency of a one-month market time is 9, the number 1 is added nine times (1·9), if the frequency of a two-month market time is 10, the number 2 is added ten times (2·10), and so on. So, to find the average market time, divide by 100 the sum of the products of each market time and its corresponding frequency. For Zip Code 1, the mean market time is 7.38 months, which by the realtor's definition of market time is an eight-month market time. For Zip Code 2, the mean market time is 12.74, which by the realtor's definition of market time is a thirteen-month market time.

The mode market time is the market time for which the frequency is the highest. For Zip Code 1, the mode market time is three months, and for Zip Code 2, the mode market time is eleven months. Therefore, the median time a house spends on the market in Zip Code 1 is less than the mean time a house spends on the market in Zip Code 1.

40. C: Children are innately curious about solving everyday problems (A); hence adults can make use of this natural characteristic by asking children to offer solutions. Once a child resolves a problem, the adult should also ask them to explain how they came to their solution. Practicing problem-solving not only teaches children to think mathematically; it also expedites language development and social skills development (B) when they work together with others. Experts advise adults not only to propose problems and ask questions about them to children, but also to have children do these things themselves (D). This gives them practice in how to think through and figure out things for themselves, as well as helping them realize that many problems have multiple and varied possible solutions.

41. B: The problem does not give any information about the size of the bracelet or the spacing between any of the charms. Nevertheless, creating a simple illustration which shows the order of the charms will help when approaching this problem. For example, the circle below represents the bracelet, and the dotted line between A and B represents the clasp. On the right, the line shows the stretched out bracelet and possible positions of charms C, D, and E based on the parameters.

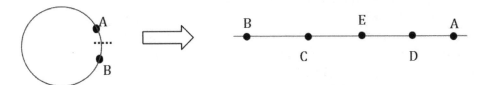

From the drawing above, it appears that statement I is true, but it is not necessarily so. The alternative drawing below also shows the charms ordered correctly, but the distance between B and E is now less than that between D and A.

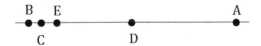

Statement II must be true: charm E must lie between B and D. Statement III must also be true: the distance between charms E and D must be less than that between C and A, which includes charms E and D in the space between them.

42. C: A number that is divisible by 6 is divisible by 2 and 3. For example, the number 12 is divisible by 2 and 3. A number ending in 6, a number with the last two digits divisible by 6 and a number with the last digit divisible by 2 or 3 is not necessarily divisible by 6; for example, 16 and 166 are not divisible by 6.

43. C: Printed mathematical formulas are an example of abstract mathematical concepts presented abstractly. Young children cannot access such concepts in abstract presentations. However, they can learn to understand abstract concepts when they are presented using concrete manipulatives like tangrams for shape recognition (A), or for reproducing and designing patterns, solving spatial problems, etc.; large, magnetized numbers and number boards (B) for doing math computations concretely; play money and toy cash registers (D) for monetary numerical activities; linking cubes, color tiles; and many other math manipulatives, which are available for teachers/schools to purchase, and/or which teachers can create in homemade versions using common found objects.

44. B: Young children learn to count to three before they have learned all of the numbers' names; then they learn to count to five, etc. Thus, they do not know all number names before learning to count (A). Children's number sense does not equate to counting alone (C). It also includes understanding various applications of numbers—not only for describing quantities (D), but also for expressing and manipulating information, and for depicting relationships among things. Children who have developed good number sense can understand these functions as well as count, and they can count forward and backward, dismantle and reassemble numbers, and add and subtract them. These abilities facilitate their developing all other math skills.

45. C: The surface area of a rectangular prism may be calculated using the formula $SA = 2lw + 2wh + 2hl$. Substituting the dimensions of 14 inches, 6 inches, and 8 inches gives $SA = 2(14)(6) + 2(6)(8) + 2(8)(14)$. Thus, the surface area is 488 square inches.

46. D: Since they are not mutually exclusive events, the probability may be written as $P(P \text{ or } T) = P(P) + P(T) - P(P \text{ and } T)$. Because the events are independent, $P(P \text{ and } T) = P(P) \times P(T)$. Substituting the probability of each event gives $(P \text{ or } T) = \frac{1}{2} + \frac{1}{2} - \left(\frac{1}{2} \times \frac{1}{2}\right) = \frac{3}{4}$.

47. A: When adults count real environmental objects together with children and also encourage children to count things themselves, they help children understand numbers through the relevant medium of their own experiences with real-life items; to understand abstract numerical concepts through concrete objects; and to get needed practice with counting and numbers. Sorting objects by their colors, shapes, and sizes *is* also relevant to helping children develop numeracy skills (B). Adults should engage children in sorting objects by *both* difference (C) and similarity (D), which helps them understand describing quantities and relationships.

48. B: It is vital for young children and all students to learn the concept that one problem can have multiple and various solutions in order to develop good problem-solving skills. This applies to solving math problems: not all math questions have only one possible right answer (A). Developing problem-solving skill is crucial to *all* parts of mathematics, not only certain ones (C). Mathematical and educational experts have found that problem-solving skills must be learned by doing, through much practice, and cannot be mastered without this practice (D).

49. C: Once children understand patterns and relationships in general, they can then understand how to categorize things because they comprehend the relationships of shared characteristics, e.g., these are all vegetables, these are all animals, etc. Understanding patterns IS related to children's understanding repetition (A), because patterns consist of regular repetitions. Patterns and relationships also DO inform understanding of rhythm (B)—e.g., differentiating longer/shorter durations of sounds or movements, identifying patterns of repeating and alternating durations, etc. This understanding IS the knowledge that enables children to order things from smallest to largest, shortest to longest (D), etc., because they comprehend the relationships that this is smaller/bigger than that, etc.

50. C: The distance may be calculated using the distance formula, $d = \sqrt{(x_2 - x_1)^2 + (y_2 - y_1)^2}$. Substituting the given coordinates, the following equation may be written: $d = \sqrt{(4 - (-8))^2 + (3 - 6)^2}$, which simplifies to $d = \sqrt{153}$.

51. B: $A \cup B$ means "A union B," or all of the elements in either of the two sets. "A union B" represents "A or B," that is, an element is in the union of A and B if it is in A *or* it is in B. The elements in sets A and B are 9, 4, −3, 8, 6, 0, −4, and 2.

52. D: Since there are 100 cm in a meter, on a 1:100 scale drawing, each centimeter represents one meter. Therefore, an area of one square centimeter on the drawing represents one square meter in actuality. Since the area of the room in the scale drawing is 30 cm², the room's actual area is 30 m².

53. B: When a child counts how many dots of one color there are in a fabric print before a different color is used, this activity is focused on identifying the pattern(s) in the print. Stringing beads with different colors in a pre-selected order (A), arranging and gluing down pieces of alternating sizes (C), and hopping on each foot for pre-determined different numbers of times (D) are all activities that are focused on *creating*, rather than *identifying*, patterns.

54. A: Young children's number sense includes, but is not limited to, understanding that we use numbers to communicate information (B), to manipulate (work with) information (C), *and* to describe quantities of things and relationships between/among things (D). Therefore, number sense encompasses understanding all of these applications of numbers.

55. D: The expression $(x - 2)^2$ may be expanded as $x^2 - 4x + 4$. Multiplication of $-3x$ by this expression gives $-3x^3 + 12x^2 - 12x$.

56. B: The sequence $\frac{1}{5}, \frac{1}{25}, \frac{1}{125}, \frac{1}{625}, \ldots$, may be used to represent the situation. Substituting the initial value of $\frac{1}{5}$ and common ratio of $\frac{1}{5}$ into the formula $S = \frac{a}{1-r}$ gives $\frac{\frac{1}{5}}{1-\frac{1}{5}}$, which simplifies to $S = \frac{\frac{1}{5}}{\frac{4}{5}}$ or $S = \frac{1}{4}$.

57. A: The net of a triangular prism has three rectangular faces and two triangular faces, and the rectangular faces must all be able to connect to each other directly.

58. B: Since they are not mutually exclusive events, the probability may be written as $P(4 \text{ or } E) = P(4) + P(E) - P(4 \text{ and } E)$. Substituting the probability of each event gives $(4 \text{ or } E) = \frac{1}{6} + \frac{1}{2} - \frac{1}{6}$, or $\frac{1}{2}$.

59. A: The standards for second-grade state that students will be able to calculate how money saved can accumulate into a larger amount over time. Defining money earned as income, which is included in the standards for first grade, is too basic for second grade. Identifying the costs and benefits of planned and unplanned spending decisions is stated in the standards for third grade. Balancing a simple budget is stated in the fifth-grade standards.

60. C: Apply the order of operations.

$$16 \div (6 - 4)^2 = 64 \qquad 8 - 2(7 - 4) = 18 \qquad 2^3 \div 2 - 2(2) = 0 \qquad 2 + 3(2^2) = 20$$
$$16 \div 2^2 = 64 \qquad 8 - 2(3) = 18 \qquad 8 \div 2 - 2(2) = 0 \qquad 2 + 3(4) = 20$$
$$16 \div 4 = 64 \qquad 8 - 6 = 18 \qquad 4 - 4 = 0 \qquad 2 + 12 = 20$$
$$4 \neq 64 \qquad 2 \neq 18 \qquad 0 = 0 \qquad 14 \neq 20$$

61. B: Claus has at most $20 to spend, so the amount he spends must be less than or equal to ($\leq$) $20. The entrance fee of $2.50 is only charged once, so it should not be multiplied by x. The cost of the entrance fee ($2.50) and the cost of the tickets ($2x$) should be added together to find the Claus's total cost of the fun fair. The correct inequality is $2.50 + 2x \leq 20$.

62. A: Since area is two dimensional, the units for area have an exponent of two such as in², yd², cm², or m².

63. B: Since the events are mutually exclusive, the sum of their individual probabilities is 1.0. Subtracting 0.6 from 1.0 yields 0.4. Therefore, the correct choice is B.

64. A: The teacher is using a concrete representation of the concept in question, since the dice she is using are a physical object which help communicate the concept. Verbal, graphic, and pictorial are not correct since the student is not merely observing a discussion about the concept or even graphic representation. Concrete representations often lead to more depth of knowledge and better retention of the concepts.

65. B: When adults ask children questions, give them time to think, and then attend to their answers, they help children learn to reason. Rather than analyzing and explaining children's own thought processes to them (A), adults do better allowing children to analyze their own thinking and then explain it. Children have this ability; encouraging them to use it gives them practice, developing their reasoning skills. They need these to understand and apply early math and science concepts, and to negotiate everyday life. Rather than tell children why something is a certain way and discussing it with them (C), adults should ask children why without expecting particular answers. This allows children to think for themselves; adults should listen to their ideas. Adults should encourage children to use logic to classify things rather than doing it for them (D). While occasional examples can help get struggling children started, it is generally better if adults invite children to use their existing logical abilities.

66. D: The table shows the y-intercept to be –5. The slope is equal to the ratio of change in y-values to change in corresponding x-values. As each x-value increases by 1, each y-value increases by 3. Thus, the slope is $\frac{3}{1}$, or 3. This graph represents the equation $y = 3x - 5$.

Science

67. B: When young children fit pegs into matching holes, or distribute one item to each child in their group, they are developing 1:1 correspondence concepts. When they see how many coins are in a piggy bank or how many children are in their group (A), they are developing counting concepts. When they divide objects into piles of the same type or shape (C), they are developing classification concepts. When they transfer sand, rice, water, or other substances from one container to others with different sizes and shapes (D), they are developing measurement concepts.

68. B: The first step in the scientific method is to ask a research question to which we want to find an answer. The second step is to formulate a hypothesis (A), which is an educated guess about the answer to the research question. The third step is to conduct an experiment (C) to test the hypothesis. The final steps are to decide whether the results of the experiment prove or disprove the hypothesis, and then to report this to others (D).

69. C: When children conduct simple experiments and are able to see patterns and meanings in the results, they are using the scientific process skill of inference. They use the skill of measurement (A) when they quantify the various physical properties of objects, like length, width, height, weight, etc. They use the skill of classification (B) when they group objects, events, conditions, or situations according to the properties they share in common. They use the skill of prediction (D) when they apply their experiences from experimenting to form new hypotheses to test.

70. C: Chemical sedimentary rocks are formed from deposits of minerals, as when flooding introduces water, which has minerals dissolved in it, and then the water evaporates, leaving behind layers of precipitated minerals no longer in solution without the water. Limestone is a chemical sedimentary rock, as are gypsum and rock salt. Clastic (A) sedimentary rock forms from clasts or little bits of rock that are compacted and cemented together. Organic (B) sedimentary rock forms from organic material like calcium from the bones and shells of animals. Pegmatite (D) is not a type of sedimentary rock; it is an intrusive igneous rock formed underground from cooling volcanic magma.

71. C: When building block structures and then dismantling them, children learn concepts of part-whole relations. They learn concepts of shape (A) when they realize that some objects roll away from them and others do not. They learn concepts of weight (B) when they try to lift different objects and find some are heavier and some lighter. As babies, they quickly learn concepts of temporal sequences (D) when they awaken wet and/or hungry and then their parents change and/or feed them. As toddlers, they also learn temporal concepts through playing, tiring, and sleeping.

72. D: Power = work / time. The mass of the object (10 kg) and the distance (10 m) can be used to calculate work. The value for time is also provided.

73. B: Gradualism states that evolution occurs slowly, with organisms exhibiting small changes over long periods of time. According to gradualism, the fossil record should show gradual changes over time. Punctuated equilibrium states that evolution occurs in spurts of sudden change. According to punctuated equilibrium, the fossil record should have large gaps.

74. D: When the electrons are strongly bound to the atoms of a substance, these atoms seldom release their electrons and thus do not conduct electricity well; such materials are electrical insulators—e.g., air, wood, glass, plastic, cotton, and ceramics. Metals and other substances whose atoms have free electrons that can separate from the atoms and move about are electrical conductors; electrical current flows freely through materials with loose electrons.

75. C: The amount that a transparent medium slows down the speed of light through it is called the index of refraction. The normal line (A) is an imaginary line that runs at a right angle to the surface of a medium; in the example given, it would be the waterline in the glass of water. The wavelength (B) of the light becomes shorter in proportion to how much the speed of light is slowed by the medium (but the medium does not change the frequency of the light wave, which is a property of the light source). The angle of refraction (D) is the degree to which the light wave is bent by the medium. As an example of refraction indices, diamonds trap light and slow its speed more than water because they are much denser and harder than water; thus, they sparkle more than water does and have a higher index of refraction than water.

76. A: The reason the sky looks blue to us is because the earth's atmosphere absorbs the wavelengths of all colors of light in the spectrum except for the wavelengths of the color blue, which it reflects back so that we see it. Therefore (B) is incorrect. Glass appears transparent to us; however, it is really only transparent to the light frequencies (wavelengths) that we can see, but to ultraviolet light frequencies, which we cannot see, glass is actually opaque. Wood, metal, and other materials look opaque to us *not* because they reflect light (D), but rather because they absorb light.

77. A: Through gills. Animals of the phylum Mollusca respire through gills. Respiration is the process of taking in oxygen and releasing carbon dioxide. Mollusks include five classes that include species as diverse as chitons, land and marine snails, and squid. This represents a diverse range of body structures. Many mollusks have a mantle that includes a cavity that is used for both breathing and excretion. Within the mantle are gills (ctenidia). Mollusks do not have tracheas. Some land snails have reduced gills that feature a respiratory cavity but are not true lungs. Muscle contraction is not required for ventilation of the gills. Other structures, such as cilia, work to pass water over the gills.

78. A: Water vapor is a gas, i.e., the gaseous form of water, which is a liquid at standard temperatures and pressures.

79. A: Liquids (C), gases (D), and plasma (B) are fluids. They share certain properties, e.g., not keeping any shape and spreading indefinitely outside of containers. Solids (A) are not fluids because they have specific atomic structures that are crystalline or three-dimensional, and specific melting points. Solids have the most cohesive molecules; gases have the least cohesive molecules; and liquids have molecules in between solids and gases in cohesion. Plasma is considered distinct from gas, due to the charges placed on the atoms, but it shares many of the properties of gases.

80. A: The purpose of conducting an experiment is to test a hypothesis. Choices B, C, and D are steps in conducting an experiment designed to test a hypothesis.

81. D: A complete metamorphosis, as butterflies undergo, includes the stages of egg (A), larva (B), pupa (D), and imago (C) or adult form. Insects such as mosquitos, grasshoppers, dragonflies, and cockroaches undergo an incomplete metamorphosis: they do not go through the stage of a pupa, which is typically inactive, does not feed, and stays hidden until the adult (imago) stage. The butterfly pupa, protected by a cocoon, is called a chrysalis. The mosquito pupa is called a tumbler.

82. B: The Earth rotates on its axis and revolves or orbits around the Sun. One complete *rotation* of the Earth on its axis equals one day (A) as we measure it. One complete *revolution* of the Earth around the Sun equals one year as we measure it. Months (C) are not associated with Earth's movements relative to the sun, but have been associated with the moon's phases as a satellite orbiting the Earth by those using lunar calendars. (The calendar most of us currently use features months slightly longer than lunar phases.) The Earth takes a year, not 100 years or a century (D), to orbit the Sun once.

83. B: In mutualistic ecological relationships, both involved organisms receive a benefit. For example, bacteria living in termites' digestive systems break down the cellulose in the wood that the termites eat, which the termites' digestive systems alone cannot do. In return for this nutritional aid, the bacteria receive a home and nourishment from the termites. In commensalistic relationships (A), one involved organism benefits while the other is unaffected; e.g., barnacles on whales are aided in their filter-feeding by the currents created in the water by the whales' swimming, while the whales are neither harmed nor helped by the barnacles. In parasitic relationships (C), one organism benefits but the other suffers. Common examples include fleas and tapeworms, which derive nourishment from animals, but harm the animals by robbing them of blood (fleas) and nutrition (tapeworms) and causing tissue damage and discomfort. Therefore (D) is incorrect.

Social Studies

84. B: Most infants typically develop the behavior of sharing activities with their peers, most notably activities involving toys or other concrete objects, by the age of one year. They have usually developed the motor and cognitive skills to walk and talk by the time they are two years old, enabling them to coordinate their behaviors while they play with their peers (A). From around three to five years old, children's development of the understanding of symbolic representation increases, as evidenced by their increasing engagement in "make-believe" scenarios (D) and pretend play. So, too, do their prosocial behaviors of helping and caring for others (C) increase during this early childhood period.

85. B: Baumrind designated Authoritative as the ideal parenting style for combining assertiveness and forgiveness; using discipline that is supportive rather than punitive; setting rules, but also explaining reasons for rules to children; being warm, nurturing, and responsive but also setting limits and boundaries; and democratically receiving, considering, and addressing children's viewpoints rather than ignoring them. Baumrind described the Authoritarian (A) style as directive, demanding, punitive, strict, and unresponsive. These parents make rules without explaining them and are not as warm or nurturing. She described the Uninvolved (C) style as one that makes neither demands nor responses. These parents meet children's basic needs, but are otherwise detached and uncommunicative. In the extreme, they can reject or neglect children. Permissive (D) parents are warm, nurturing, responsive, and communicative, but do not set rules and limits or discipline children.

86. B: When a dominant culture absorbs other cultures so that they all adopt all the behaviors of the dominant culture, this is called assimilation: the dominant culture assimilates other cultures.

When different ethnic groups unite to form a new culture, this is also assimilation, not acculturation (A). The adoption by one culture of some of another culture's traits is acculturation, not assimilation (C). When two or more different cultures virtually fuse, this is also a type of acculturation rather than assimilation (D).

87. C: Native American and Asian cultures tend to be collectivist; i.e., they value interdependence among people, relationships, and social interactions. Latin American and African cultures also are more likely to embrace collectivism, focusing on the common good more than individual achievement; thus (A) is incorrect. Individualism, however, is *more* common in Canadian and Australian cultures, not less; so (B) is incorrect. European and North American cultures also favor individual expression, self-determination, independence, uniqueness, and self-actualization; hence they are more individualistic cultures, not more collectivist, so (D) is incorrect.

88. A: The eye wall of a hurricane has the strongest winds and the greatest rainfall. The eye wall is the tower-like rim of the eye. It is from this wall that clouds extend out, which are seen from above as the classic outward spiral pattern. A hurricane front is the outermost edge of its influence; although there will be heavy winds and rain in this area, the intensity will be relatively small. The eye of a hurricane is actually a place of surprising peace. In this area, dry and cool air rushes down to the ground or sea. Once there, the air is caught up in the winds of the eye wall and is driven outward at a furious pace.

89. D: The first level of EC self-awareness is differentiation, wherein children realize their reflections in mirrors are making the same movements they are, and they can tell their mirror reflections apart from other people, showing differentiation of self. The second level is situation, wherein children understand that their mirror reflections are unique to the self, and that their selves, bodies, and other things are physically situated in space. The third level is identification, wherein children can identify their mirror reflections as "me." When they see a mark on their faces by looking at a mirror, they reach for their own faces rather than for the mirror image. The fourth level is permanence, wherein children realize a permanent self, recognizing themselves in photographs and videos despite their different ages, places, clothing, etc. in these records. The fifth level is self-consciousness, also called meta-self-awareness, wherein children can see the self from the perspectives of others as well as from their own.

90. A: Popular approaches to conflict resolution for early childhood ages (e.g., the HighScope program) are typically very similar in their steps to the steps used in adult conflict mediation. When adults intervene in a conflict among young children, they are advised to listen to children's feelings, and also to acknowledge these rather than not saying anything (B). Adults should not only gather information from the children about their conflict, but should also restate the problem identified by the children rather than not talking about it (C). Suggesting possible solutions is something an adult should ask the children to do themselves rather than doing it for them (D); the adult should then help the children come to an agreement about which solution they choose. Adults should follow up with support as needed.

91. C: According to family systems theory, boundaries pertain to what a family includes and excludes, its limits, and its relative levels of togetherness and separation. Characteristics of disengaged families include *less* restricted or closed boundaries rather than vice versa (A); valuing independence more highly than enmeshed families do rather than vice versa (B); and being more open to considering new input (C). Characteristics of enmeshed families include having more restricted or closed boundaries than disengaged families, rather than looser and more flexible ones (D), and valuing togetherness, belonging, and loyalty more than autonomy.

92. C: In cartography, the scale of miles on a map enables us to estimate actual distances between places. For example, a map's scale of miles may state that one inch equals 500 miles. Thus, a ratio is required to interpret this information: by measuring with a ruler, if we see that the distance on the map between two cities, states, or countries equals six inches, then we can estimate the actual distance between these locations to be 3,000 miles. The key or legend (A) on a map identifies what the different symbols and colors used in the map indicate. The compass rose (B) on a map shows north, south, east, and west directions so we can see the orientations of different places. The lines in a grid (D) on a map indicate latitudes, or parallels, which run east-west, and longitudes, or meridians, which run north-south. By finding the intersection of latitude and longitude coordinates for a given place, we can determine its absolute location.

93. C: One geographical concept is distance. For example, product prices are affected by the cost of transportation, which in turn is affected by how far away raw materials are from the factories that process them, and prices for land closer to highways are higher than for land farther away from them. Location is another geography concept. Absolute location is determined by a place's latitude and longitude, not land prices (A). Relative location is determined by a region's changing characteristics, which surrounding areas can influence; one example is that land costs more in urban than rural areas. Relative location is not determined by latitude and longitude (B). Achievability is related to the accessibility of a geographical area; for example, villages with surrounding forests or swamps are less accessible than those on beaches. The dependency of an area, and hence its achievability, *does* change (D) as its technology, transportation, and economy change.

94. B: Permissive parents are nurturing, responsive, and communicative with their children. However, they avoid confronting and/or disciplining children and do not expect them to demonstrate much self-control or maturity. Consequently, their children tend to have problems with authority figures, poor school performance, and deficits in self-regulation. The children of unresponsive, overly strict, demanding, harshly punitive authoritarian (A) parents tend to develop proficient technical and school performance and obedience, but lack social skills, self-esteem, and happiness. The children of authoritative (C) parents, who have the ideal parenting style, tend to develop competence, success, and happiness. Uninvolved (D) parents, who are undemanding but also unresponsive, uncommunicative, and detached, and may even neglect or reject children, produce children lacking competence, self-esteem, and self-control.

95. A: Historically, slave owners did not permit the African slaves they bought to learn how to read and write. Though some slaves still managed secretly to attain literacy, the majority suffered forced illiteracy and thus developed a rich oral tradition of storytelling, songs, etc., which they transmitted to succeeding generations. Latin American culture has had a significant influence on North American music and dance (B), as evidenced in the growing popularity of Latino music within North American popular music, and in the Latin division of ballroom dancing. Recent Asian immigrants do not all immediately adopt American family structures (C); when arriving in America, extended families (grandparents, aunts, uncles, cousins, etc.) are more likely to continue living together. The policies of European-American settlers have eradicated much of Native Americans' tribal culture (D); while some groups have worked hard to preserve their tribal languages, religions, music, dance, artwork, and other customs, overall much of their culture has been lost along with much of their population.

96. A: Political socialization occurs when people are made aware of political culture, facts, and values. Family, friends, society, and the media influence political socialization. Sex, race, age, education, income, and region are also indicators of how a person will vote.

97. A: After approaching calmly, stopping any behaviors that cause physical or emotional harm (step 1), and acknowledging the children's feelings (step 2), the third step in this conflict-mediation/resolution process* is to accumulate as much information as is necessary about the particular conflict from the involved parties. The fourth step is for the mediator to reiterate or restate what the problem is (C). The fifth step is to ask the involved children to think of and suggest potential solutions to the problem identified, and then help them agree to one selected solution (B). The sixth step is to follow up the conflict resolution by providing the involved parties with whatever support they need (D). *[from the HighScope Educational Research Foundation]

98. C: Babies typically develop the self-awareness ability to differentiate between live video of themselves and people imitating their behaviors around four to seven months of age. Newborns (A) demonstrate the self-awareness ability of differentiating their bodies from the environment and internal/self from external/other stimulation from birth. Two-year-olds (B) demonstrate awareness of symbolic representation, understanding that mirror images and photos represent themselves. Babies typically regularly reach for things they see around four months of age. Around four to six months (D) of age, babies are able to regulate their reaching movements according to their postural and balance levels.

99. C: The geographical concept of Interaction (A) refers to interdependent and mutual relationships between different geographic areas. For example, urban areas depend on the raw materials (e.g., ores from mines or plant crops) from rural areas for industrial manufacturing, and rural areas depend on urban ones both as markets for their raw materials, and for the industrial products they make. The concept of Spatial Interrelatedness (D) refers to the relationship of physical and nonphysical aspects, such as the rural and urban areas described here. The concept of Area Differentiation (B) refers to differences in aspects of regional geography, e.g., how altitude and climate influence which plants are grown, and regional influences on differences in occupations, e.g., farming or fishing.

100. C: One reason for laws and rules that we can communicate to young children to help them understand important civics concepts is that they confer greater predictability, order, and security to our society and hence our lives. Another reason is that laws and rules identify for citizens which behaviors are acceptable and which are unacceptable, rather than only punishing the latter (A). Another reason is that laws and rules delegate various responsibilities to citizens, rather than interfering with these (B). An additional reason is that laws and rules *limit* the power of persons in authority positions to prevent them from abusing their positions, rather than increasing that power (D).

Arts

101. B: Form is an artistic element that would only apply to three-dimensional art forms, such as sculptures or decorative arts. Two-dimensional works of art have the element of shape, which refers to their length and width, while three-dimensional works of art have the element of form, which refers to their length, width, and depth. Proportion and balance are both *principles* of art that would apply to both two- and three-dimensional works. Line is an artistic element that would be applicable to both types of art.

102. B: If the class unit is on space travel, then an art activity of constructing models of rocket ships would integrate art thematically into the curriculum more than painting portraits of classmates (A), exploring different art materials all in one color (C), or using art work to express their feelings (D) would. Assigning art projects focused on the same themes that are central to their curriculum units and/or lessons is one way that teachers can integrate art across academic content areas.

103. A: Visual literacy can best be described as the ability to communicate through images and comprehend the messages contained in images. In visual literacy education, students are taught not only to create images that appropriately communicate information but also to interpret and derive meaning from both artistic and informational images.

104. A: The activity described will help children learn about the role of line in visual art, and also about how to draw different kinds of lines. They will also learn how to use different art tools for drawing lines. The children will learn more from this activity using their own body outlines than one using other shapes (B), because young children prefer activities where they are the focus over activities that do not relate to themselves. The children will also learn about shape, but not more than they will learn about line (C), which is the primary focus of this activity. The children may also learn kinesthetic concepts from posing their bodies in different creative positions, but they will definitely learn about art (D) by learning about line and different kinds of lines, about shape and drawing, and about different art tools for making lines.

105. C: In 3/4 time, the quarter note is selected as the one beat unit, while in 6/8 time the eighth note is used. Essentially, 6/8 time is the same as the six-note form of 3/4. The only difference is that the eighth note is used as the one-beat unit.

106. A: Artists will often use portfolios to demonstrate their capabilities. Portfolios are not designed to communicate past work history or education and are rarely used for teaching purposes. The intention of a portfolio is not to showcase an artist's entire body of work, but instead to highlight select pieces. A portfolio is also not intended to lay claim to copyright privileges.

107. D: Johannes Brahms, who composed music in the middle to late 19th century. Therefore, Brahms is most strongly associated with the Romantic Period in classical music, which ran from about 1815 to about 1910. Bach is most strongly associated with the Baroque Period (1600-1760), and Ravel is most closely associated with the Impressionist Period (1890-1940). Aaron Copland, often is considered "the dean of American composers" and composed music in the mid to late 20th century; he would not fit into any of the above listed periods.

108. B: In fact, the majority of artists hold postsecondary degrees or certificates. More than half of artists are self-employed, and competition is keen for salaried jobs in the art industry. Annual earnings for artists vary widely, according to the Bureau of Labor Statistics.

109. B: A fresco is actually a painting style that involves applying paint or pigment directly to plaster. In order to give pigment the desired consistency for fluid painting, several things can be mixed with the pigment: A tempera such as oil, egg, or water; turpentine, which is used as a cleaner and thinner; and an oil medium, which has opposite effects as turpentine, making the paint fatter.

110. D: The organizing principle of unity in art means the work is cohesive; all of its elements seem to belong together, and combine into a completed whole in our perceptions. We may perceive artworks lacking unity as disorganized, fragmented, incomplete, and/or as collections of disconnected parts. The organizing principle of repetition (A) in art means the artist repeats certain elements—e.g., musical themes or motifs; certain visual lines, shapes, colors, textures, etc.; certain dance steps or step combinations; or certain dramatic actions or lines of dialogue— throughout the piece to create structure, emphasis, and change to achieve desired effects. The organizing principle of contrast (B) in art means the artist combines noticeable differences in the work's elements to create interest and excitement and avoid monotony. The organizing principle of balance (C) in art means the artist achieves visual, aural, kinetic, and/or dramatic equilibrium among the various elements used in the work. Balance also contributes to unity.

Health and Physical Education

111. D: Joints are the junctions of bones, i.e., the places where bones connect or meet with each other. Ligaments (A) are bands of fibrous connective tissue that connect the bones, forming joints. Tendons (B) are elastic connective tissues that connect the muscles to the bones. Cartilage (C) is fibrous connective tissue that covers the surfaces of bones to keep them from rubbing against and damaging one another.

112. A: The Babinski reflex occurs when the sole of the foot is firmly stroked vertically: the big toe moves upward and the other toes fan outward. This is normal in newborns and disappears anytime between 1 and 2 years of age. The stepping reflex (B), wherein newborns automatically perform a stepping motion when held upright with their feet on or near a surface, typically disappears around the age of 2 months. The palmar grasping reflex (C), wherein a baby will grasp an offered adult finger in his or her fist, typically disappears around 3–4 months. The tonic reflex (D), wherein newborns assume the "fencing position" with the head turned to one side, one arm in front of the eyes and the other arm bent at the elbow, typically disappears around the age of 4 months.

113. B: Many older homes have lead water pipes. Running hot water can dissolve lead into the water, resulting in unacceptable levels of this toxic heavy metal in drinking water. Therefore, parents should prepare baby formula using only cold water. House dust IS considered a health risk (A); dust mites can trigger allergy symptoms including asthma, and these can be serious. Indoor CO gas often occurs, but is NOT normal OR harmless (C): CO poisoning indoors can kill pets and sicken or kill humans. While people do need some sunlight, sun exposure IS a risk (D): babies should be kept out of direct sunlight, and young children should be protected with sunscreen and sun-protective clothing, because unprotected sun exposure causes skin damage and can lead to skin cancer.

114. D: Malnutrition is not only caused by eating too little; it is also caused by eating foods that are not nutritious, eating unbalanced diets, and not getting enough of all necessary nutrients. Thus, people can eat too much and become overweight, but if most of the calories they consume are "empty", i.e., they contain few or no vitamins, minerals, protein, healthy fats, or fiber, they can suffer malnutrition. In fact, overconsumption of refined carbohydrates that lack fiber instead of whole grains; saturated and trans fats instead of monounsaturated and polyunsaturated fats; and processed foods instead of fruits and vegetables contribute to both obesity and malnutrition. Anxiety, depression, and other emotional factors can not only disrupt sleeping and eating, but also cause high blood pressure and heart disease (A). Stress and family dysfunction can cause both emotional and physical illness (B). Air pollution is found both to aggravate and to cause asthma (C).

115. A: The American Recovery and Reinvestment Act, among other provisions, allotted funds to prevent chronic disease as a way to promote wellness. This initiative targets obesity and tobacco use as the two most preventable causes of disability and death in America today. Alcohol use {(B), (C)} and the abuse of alcohol and other drugs (D) are not considered as prevalent or as preventable as obesity and the use of tobacco.

116. C: Babies typically can play "pattycake" between 7–15 months of age, at an average age of around 9 months. They typically can pull up to stand between 5–12 months, at an average age of around 8 months. They typically develop the pincer grasp (D) for picking up small objects between 6–12 months. Children with normal development typically can jump in place (C) between 17–30 months of age, at an average age of around 23½ months, i.e., almost two years old.

117. A: Multiple research studies repeatedly demonstrate that cardiovascular diseases, diabetes, and colon and breast cancer risks are lowered by regular physical activity (PA). Researchers recommend 30 to 60 minutes a day of PA to reduce the risks of breast and colon cancer significantly, and 150 minutes a week to decrease risks of cardiovascular diseases and diabetes. Thirty minutes a day for five days a week equals 150 minutes a week; therefore, the amounts needed are similar to lower the risks of these diseases. (Sixty minutes is double this and may afford some people greater cancer risk reduction.) Hence, risks for all these diseases are lowered, not some (B). The amounts necessary to reduce risk do not vary greatly among these diseases (C). Regular PA in adequate amounts does lower disease risk (D).

118. B: If students begin to feel overextended when they engage in extracurricular activities, it is a sign that they should quit at least one activity. Students should consider not only the abilities and skills they already have and familiar interests but also trying new things in which they are interested as well as consider the time they have available before they choose extracurricular activities.

119. C: Iron deficiencies in children have been found to cause symptoms of shortened attention spans, attentional deficits, and irritability similar to the symptoms of Attention Deficit/Hyperactivity Disorder (ADHD), as well as fatigue. Children who skip breakfast (A) have been found to perform with lower speed and accuracy than normal on problem-solving measures. Children who regularly miss meals (B) in general (not just breakfast) have been found to get sick more often and be absent from school more. Children with protein deficiencies (D) are found to have lower achievement test scores than peers getting enough protein.

120. D: The primary principle of the theory of deliberate practice is that practicing a skill needs to be a focused and reflective process. If the student is not deliberate, or focused on making progress, the student's volume of practice will not be enough to improve their skill level. A secondary principal of deliberate practice is that there needs to be much practice to see effective gains. Regardless of students' ability levels, including the ability level of those who are natural athletes, lots of practice is required to achieve mastery. Short bouts of regular practice have shown to be the most effective method of skill mastery. While some believe that practice makes perfect, performing a skill incorrectly repeatedly will negate mastery of the desired skill. "Perfect practice makes perfect" would be more appropriate.

Practice Test #2

Language Arts

1. Which component of oral language development involves the social rules for using language?

- a. The pragmatic component
- b. The phonological component
- c. The semantic component
- d. The syntactic component

2. A teacher preparing Specially Designed Academic Instruction in English (SDAIE) lessons for English language learner (ELL) students mainstreamed in an English-language class is planning small-group collaborative work to discuss their analyses and interpretations of English literature texts. What is the best way to group students for this assignment?

- a. The ELL students should be grouped homogeneously to facilitate communication.
- b. The ELL and native English-speaking students should be grouped heterogeneously.
- c. The ELL students should be grouped heterogeneously but at least two per group.
- d. The ELL and native English-speaking students' grouping will not make a difference.

3. Which of the following is true about how teachers can cultivate print awareness in young children?

- a. It is effective to have children narrate picture books and give them matching reinforcements.
- b. It is superfluous to use large-print texts for reading to younger children who cannot read yet.
- c. Teachers should label things/areas in classrooms using either pictures or words, but not both.
- d. When reading storybooks to young children, the texts should use novel, unpredictable words.

4. Which of the following phonological awareness activities is easiest for children?

- a. Naming rhyming words for a word
- b. Picking rhyming words from lists
- c. Recognizing words that rhyme
- d. These are all equally difficult.

5. The most effective strategy for decoding sight words is:

- a. Segmenting sight words into syllables. Beginning readers are understandably nervous when encountering a long word that isn't familiar. Blocking off all but a single syllable at a time renders a word manageable and allows the reader a sense of control over the act of reading
- b. Word families. By grouping the sight word with similar words, patterns emerge
- c. A phonemic approach. When students understand the connection between individual words and their sounds, they will be able to sound out any sight word they encounter
- d. None; sight words cannot be decoded. Readers must learn to recognize these words as wholes on sight

43

6. Which of these is correct regarding children's reading fluency?

    a. Sounding choppy when reading out loud indicates a lack of fluency.

    b. Fluency is only an issue for children when they are reading out loud.

    c. Reading aloud without expression is no issue as long as it is accurate.

    d. Reading fluency is measured by reading speed, but not by accuracy.

7. A teacher wants to incorporate a lesson on point of view into his class's fairy tale genre study. Which activity would best accomplish this goal?

    a. Reading a modern-day fairy tale and asking students to record what they liked and didn't like about the story in their journals

    b. Contrasting two versions of the same fairy tale narrated by two different characters

    c. Having students write a different ending to an existing fairy tale

    d. Comparing and contrasting the events in a fractured fairy tale and its traditional version

8. A teacher wants to help his students compare and contrast two main characters within a fictional story. Which graphic organizer should he use to best help students achieve this objective?

    a. Venn diagram

    b. Story map

    c. Five W's chart

    d. T-chart

9. In addition to word frequency, sentence complexity, and vocabulary, which of the following factors is frequently used to level books?

    a. Author's purpose

    b. Interest level

    c. Text features

    d. Author's craft

10. In which stage of children's writing development do they first realize that meanings are expressed by written symbols?

    a. Scribbling and drawing stage

    b. The stage with writing letters

    c. The letters and spaces stage

    d. Letter-like forms and shapes

11. Another name for a persuasive essay is:

    a. Dynamic essay

    b. Convincing essay

    c. Argumentative essay

    d. Position paper

12. Which of the following is NOT typically categorized as a prewriting process?

    a. Planning

    b. Reflection

    c. Visualization

    d. Brainstorming

13. Which of the following is most accurate regarding writing style?

a. The kind of diction you use does not affect style.
b. You add style later to give your writing personality.
c. Style is unrelated to your control of your content.
d. Your purpose for writing guides your writing style.

14. Which of the following is the best use of technology in a language arts classroom?

a. Providing laptops to students to achieve more effective note-taking, access to word processing programs, and access to the internet
b. Encouraging the use of slide shows or similar programs to support lectures and oral presentations, as well as to organize pertinent class concepts
c. Incorporating a computer-based "language lab" in which students can listen to texts and engage in interactive word-study and comprehension activities
d. Whenever possible, watching film interpretations based on texts studied in class

15. With a teacher's guidance, a class brainstorms main ideas, topics, or concepts from a text. Students choose a select number of these ideas and copy them onto separate index cards. The students then individually review the text, recording any supporting evidence on the notecard with the applicable main idea. This activity would be an excellent pre-lesson for teaching which skill set?

a. Working as a group to interpret a text and write an appropriate and realistic sequel, focusing on interpretive comprehension and creative writing.
b. Silent reading as a form of comprehension practice.
c. Organizing ideas for writing a cohesive and persuasive essay or research paper that asserts supported arguments with valid supporting evidence.
d. Literal and figurative comprehension, as well as contributing to group discussions via oral communication skills.

16. To present information clearly in a written speech, which of these applies?

a. A speechwriter need not define the purpose of a speech beforehand.
b. To interest audiences, speeches should not be organized too logically.
c. Making an outline of a speech first will result in a more boring speech.
d. Sentence structure and word choice precision must rival reading text.

17. Third-grade students typically receive their spelling word lists each Monday so that they can practice them at home before the test on Friday. While their teacher is pleased that the students usually receive high grades on spelling tests, she observes that they misspell those same words when writing in journals or doing classwork. How should this teacher modify her instruction?

a. Post a list of vocabulary words when the students are writing to help them recall correct spellings.
b. Integrate spelling words into writing, reading, grammar, phonics, and other activities to help students learn the words in a variety of contexts.
c. Provide more time, such as a two-week period, between tests so that students have more time to study.
d. Review the words before certain activities to increase immediate recall of correct spellings.

18. Which of the following sentences uses correct capitalization?

    a. "This bill was signed into law by the President."

    b. "Some of our cousins lived in Washington, D.C."

    c. "He wrote that he plans to come South to visit."

    d. "My classes include English, Science, and Math."

19. A beginning reader unfamiliar with seeing the homophones "reads" and "reeds" in print deduces the meaning of plants, not perusal, from the sentence "Reeds grow in marshes" because the former makes sense in the sentence while the latter does not. This is an example of using _____ to aid comprehension.

    a. Phonics

    b. Context

    c. Spelling

    d. Pictures

20. "It's raining cats and dogs" is an example of which type of expression?

    a. Idiom

    b. Proverb

    c. Simile

    d. Metaphor

21. Of the three tiers of words, the most important words for direct instruction are:

    a. Tier-one words

    b. Common words

    c. Tier-two words

    d. Words with Latin roots

22. Regarding the reading strategy of summarizing text, which of the following is most accurate about what will help students support their reading comprehension?

    a. It will help them to identify important ideas, but not to organize them.

    b. It will help them to identify themes, problems, and solutions in a text.

    c. It will help them to monitor comprehension more than to sequence it.

    d. It will help them to make visual the connections with text they realize.

23. In writing paragraphs, which structural pattern most often uses a chronological sequence?

    a. Compare-contrast

    b. Cause-effect

    c. Analogy

    d. Process

24. Of the following statements, which one is accurate regarding teacher promotion and management of active listening and participation by students in collaborative discussions?

    a. For students inexperienced in group discussions, teachers should use topics below their age levels.

    b. To challenge students, teachers should assign group discussion topics above their age levels.

    c. If teachers explain appropriate discussion behaviors first, modeling them becomes unnecessary.

    d. Teachers should model and explain active listening behaviors for students before discussions.

25. Which of the following statements correctly reflects one of the principles of emergent literacy theory?

    a. When young children "reread" storybooks, this means they have memorized them.

    b. Young children's invented spellings afford no information about phonetic familiarity.

    c. It is crucial for adults to read to young children, but not before they are a certain age.

    d. Reading and writing development are viewed as processes having successive stages.

26. Of the following statements, which adheres to Information Literacy standards?

    a. Students accessing information must critically evaluate it and its sources before using it.

    b. Students accessing information can ascertain how much of it they need after they find it.

    c. Students accessing information efficiently sacrifice broader scope and incidental learning.

    d. Students accessing information ethically must eschew using it to attain specific purposes.

27. Mrs. Lopez teaches second grade. After completing a science experiment, she gathers her students on the carpet to write a summary of what they learned. Mrs. Lopez asks students to help her record the responses on chart paper, sharing the marker. She provides guidance and sentence starters as needed. After everyone has recorded their responses, the class reads them aloud together. Which type of writing experience is Mrs. Lopez demonstrating?

    a. Interactive writing

    b. Shared writing

    c. Independent writing

    d. Guided writing

28. A child in kindergarten is _most_ likely to be referred to a speech-language pathologist if s/he does not correctly produce which of the following phonemes?

    a. /p/ as in pepper or poppies

    b. /ʒ/ as in mirage or measure

    c. /v/ as in velvet, valve, value

    d. /s/ as in see, yes, or asking

29. Which of the following activities requires ESL students to use conversational English rather than academic English?

    a. Understanding their school textbooks

    b. Solving mathematical word problems

    c. Understanding a teacher's questions

    d. Dealing with new/abstract concepts

30. In learning the alphabetic principle, which do children typically develop first?
- a. They learn the shapes of letters.
- b. They learn the sounds of letters.
- c. They learn these all concurrently.
- d. They learn the names of letters.

31. Of the following, which represents an indirect way in which students receive instruction in and learn vocabulary?
- a. Being exposed repeatedly to vocabulary in multiple teaching contexts
- b. Being exposed to vocabulary when adults read aloud to them
- c. Being pre-taught specific words found in text prior to reading
- d. Being taught vocabulary words over extended periods of time

32. Which of the following best explains the importance prior knowledge brings to the act of reading?
- a. Prior knowledge is information the student gets through researching a topic prior to reading the text. A student who is well-prepared through such research is better able to decode a text and retain its meaning.
- b. Prior knowledge is knowledge the student brings from previous life or learning experiences to the act of reading. It is not possible for a student to fully comprehend new knowledge without first integrating it with prior knowledge.
- c. Prior knowledge is predictive. It motivates the student to look for contextual clues in the reading and predict what is likely to happen next.
- d. Prior knowledge is not important to any degree to the act of reading because every text is self-contained and therefore seamless. Prior knowledge is irrelevant in this application.

33. Which of these is accurate about how teachers should introduce components of phonics to young children?
- a. Teachers should present words that contain a, s, h, and m first.
- b. *X* as in *box*, *gh* as in *through*, and *ey* as in *they* are of high utility.
- c. Teachers should present the consonants p, b, t, d, k, and g first.
- d. A reasonable rate is to teach 10-15 sound-letter pairs per week.

34. Examples of CVC words include:
- a. Add, pad, mad
- b. Cat, tack, act
- c. Elephant, piano, examine
- d. Dog, sit, leg

35. *Since*, *whether*, and *accordingly* are examples of which type of signal words?
- a. Common, or basic, signal words
- b. Compare/contrast words
- c. Cause–effect words
- d. Temporal sequencing words

36. The questions in this test can give you an idea of what kinds of questions you might find on the actual test; however, they are not duplicates of the actual test questions, which cover the same knowledge but may differ somewhat in form and content.

The preceding sentence is which of the following sentence types?

    a. Simple
    b. Complex
    c. Compound
    d. Compound-complex

Mathematics

37. Which of the following teacher practices can help children learn to apply the math they learn in school to everyday problem solving in real life?

    a. Emphasize the view of mathematics as a discipline composed of rules and procedures.
    b. Work to form connections between children's intuitive math thinking and formal math.
    c. Avoid introducing concrete objects to manipulate when teaching formal mathematics.
    d. Omit real-life examples of math concepts or math vocabulary describing child activities.

38. Which of these examples of symbolic representation and emerging math skills in children typically develops at the *latest* (oldest) ages?

    a. Drawing pictures and maps
    b. Counting using their fingers
    c. Making graphs to show data
    d. Making tallies using tick-marks

39. What is the midpoint of the line segment below?

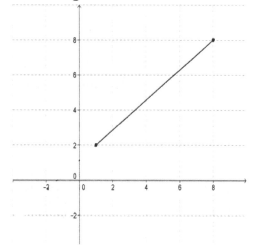

    a. $(3.5, 4)$
    b. $(4, 4)$
    c. $(4.5, 5)$
    d. $(5, 5)$

40. Ann must walk from Point A to Point B and then to Point C. Finally, she will walk back to Point A. If each unit represents 5 miles, which of the following best represents the total distance she will have walked?

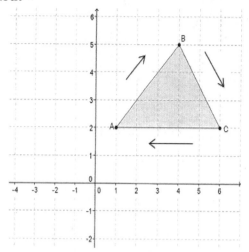

    a. 42 miles
    b. 48 miles
    c. 56 miles
    d. 64 miles

41. Which of these is true about the use of manipulatives for EC math learning?
    a. Manipulatives are so effective for learning that some early math curricula require these.
    b. Manipulatives help preschoolers with visual/haptic learning styles but not other children.
    c. Manipulatives can help preschoolers learn concrete things rather than abstract concepts.
    d. Manipulatives are fun, but preschoolers do not learn by seeing/touching/moving objects.

42. Two companies offer monthly cell phone plans, both of which include free text messaging. Company A charges a $25 monthly fee plus five cents per minute of phone conversation, while Company B charges a $50 monthly fee and offers unlimited calling. Both companies charge the same amount when the total duration of monthly calls is
    a. 500 hours.
    b. 8 hours and 33 minutes.
    c. 8 hours and 20 minutes.
    d. 5 hours.

43. Solve the system of equations.

$$3x + 4y = 2$$
$$2x + 6y = -2$$

    a. $\left(0, \frac{1}{2}\right)$
    b. $\left(\frac{2}{5}, \frac{1}{5}\right)$
    c. $(2, -1)$
    d. $\left(-1, \frac{5}{4}\right)$

44. Identify the cross-section polygon formed by a plane containing the given points on the cube.

    a. Rectangle
    b. Trapezoid
    c. Pentagon
    d. Hexagon

45. Of the following, which most helps young children connect mathematics to real life?

    a. Formal math instruction in school
    b. Describing activities in math words
    c. Using novel manipulatives in math
    d. Original examples of new concepts

46. Jason decides to donate 1% of his annual salary to a local charity. If his annual salary is $45,000, how much will he donate?

    a. $4.50
    b. $45
    c. $450
    d. $4,500

47. Kevin saves $3 during Month 1. During each subsequent month, he plans to save 4 more dollars than he saved during the previous month. Which of the following equations represents the amount he will save during the nth month?

    a. $a_n = 3n - 1$
    b. $a_n = 3n + 4$
    c. $a_n = 4n + 3$
    d. $a_n = 4n - 1$

48. A tree with a height of 15 feet casts a shadow that is 5 feet in length. A man standing at the base of the shadow formed by the tree is 6 feet tall. How long is the shadow cast by the man?

    a. 1.5 feet
    b. 2 feet
    c. 2.5 feet
    d. 3 feet

49. The simulation of a coin toss is completed 300 times. Which of the following best represents the number of tosses you can expect to show heads?

    a. 50
    b. 100
    c. 150
    d. 200

50. Mr. Mancelli teaches math. He is making prize bags for the winners of a math game. If he has eight candy bars and twelve packages of gum, what is the largest number of identical prize bags he can make without having any left-over candy bars or packages of gum?

    a. 2
    b. 4
    c. 6
    d. 8

51. Which of the following goals is appropriate in the category of algebraic reasoning for first-grade students?

    a. Students represent one- and two-step problems involving addition and subtraction of whole numbers to 1,000 using pictorial models, number lines, and equations.
    b. Students represent real-world relationships using number pairs in a table and verbal descriptions.
    c. Students represent word problems involving addition and subtraction of whole numbers up to 20 using concrete and pictorial models and number sentences.
    d. Students recite numbers up to at least 100 by ones and tens beginning with any given number.

52. Which of the following descriptions best fits a hexagonal prism?

    a. 8 faces, 18 edges, 12 vertices
    b. 6 faces, 18 edges, 12 vertices
    c. 8 faces, 16 edges, 8 vertices
    d. 6 faces, 14 edges, 10 vertices

53. Addison tosses a six-sided die twelve times and records the results in the table below.

Toss	1	2	3	4	5	6	7	8	9	10	11	12
Results	2	5	1	2	3	6	6	2	4	5	4	3

Which of the following statements is true?

    a. The experimental probability of tossing a 6 is greater than the theoretical probability.
    b. The experimental probability of tossing a 3 is greater than the theoretical probability.
    c. The experimental probability of tossing a 1 is greater than the theoretical probability.
    d. The experimental probability of tossing a 2 is greater than the theoretical probability.

54. If $f(x) = \frac{x^3 - 2x + 1}{3x}$, what is $f(2)$?

    a. $\frac{1}{3}$
    b. $\frac{1}{2}$
    c. $\frac{5}{6}$
    d. $\frac{5}{2}$

55. A developer decides to build a fence around a neighborhood park, which is positioned on a rectangular lot. Rather than fencing along the lot line, he fences _x_ feet from each of the lot's boundaries. By fencing a rectangular space 141 yd^2 smaller than the lot, the developer saves $432 in fencing materials, which cost $12 per linear foot. How much does he spend?

    a. $160
    b. $456
    c. $3,168
    d. The answer cannot be determined from the given information.

56. Which of the following is true about representation skills relative to young children?

    a. Children will not develop representation skills until they are older.
    b. Children are not using representation when they count on fingers.
    c. Children draw pictures because they have no representation skills.
    d. Children show representation in make-believe play and tally marks.

57. How can a teacher help a young child apply math process skills during typical preschool activities?

    a. When a child sorts toys by color, the teacher describes this as classification.
    b. When a child sorts toys by color, the teacher asks how s/he is sorting them.
    c. When a child sorts toys by color, the teacher asks how else s/he might sort.
    d. When a child sorts toys by color, these all apply varying math process skills.

58. Which of the following statements is true of the following data?

Test scores by class

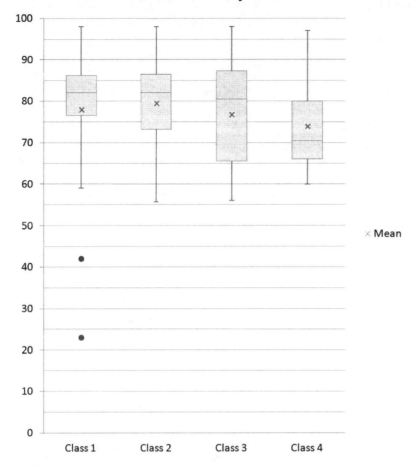

a. The mean better reflects student performance in Class 1 than the median.
b. The mean test score for Class 1 and 2 is the same.
c. The median test score for Class 1 and 2 is the same.
d. The median test score is above the mean for Class 4.

59. Marcus is mowing yards and doing odd jobs to earn money for a new video game system that costs $325. Marcus only charges $6.50 per hour. Which of the following equations represents the number of hours Marcus needs to work to earn $325?

a. $6.50x = 325$
b. $6.50 + x = 325$
c. $325x = 6.50$
d. $6.50x + 325 = x$

60. A dartboard consists of two concentric circles with radii of 3 inches and 6 inches. If a dart is thrown onto the board, what is the probability the dart will land in the inner circle?

    a. $\frac{1}{4}$

    b. $\frac{1}{2}$

    c. $\frac{1}{3}$

    d. $\frac{1}{5}$

61. Of the following examples of preschooler behaviors, which one is developmentally normal and typical, but less an example of using mathematical concepts than the others?

    a. A child collects three of his toys, looks at them, and says, "I have three toys here."
    b. A child sees three toys, holds up three fingers, and says, "This is how many toys."
    c. A child with two cookies says, "If you give me one more cookie, I will have three."
    d. A child with two cookie halves says, "I have more than" a child with a whole cookie.

62. Which of these is the most valid advice for adults in playing mental math games with young children?

    a. It is important for the adult and child to take turns posing and solving story problems.
    b. It is more important for the adult to give the child correct answers than ask questions.
    c. It is more important for the game to be strictly factual, like most math tests, than fun.
    d. It is important to give children unknown variable or number games in early childhood.

63. Very young children naturally think about mathematical concepts in ways that are primarily:

    a. Formal.
    b. Logical.
    c. Intuitive.
    d. Deductive.

64. A ball has a diameter of 7 inches. Which of the following best represents the volume?

    a. 165.7 in^3
    b. 179.6 in^3
    c. 184.5 in^3
    d. 192.3 in^3

65. Which of the following pairs of equations represents the lines of symmetry in the figure below?

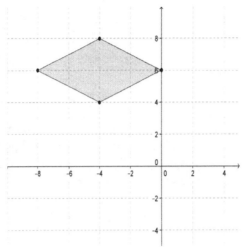

a. $x = -4, y = 6$
b. $x = 4, y = 6$
c. $y = -4, x = 6$
d. $y = 4, x = -6$

66. Which of these graphs is NOT representative of the data set shown below?

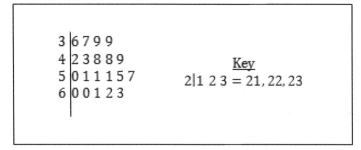

```
3 | 6 7 9 9
4 | 2 3 8 8 9          Key
5 | 0 1 1 1 5 7    2|1 2 3 = 21, 22, 23
6 | 0 0 1 2 3
```

a.

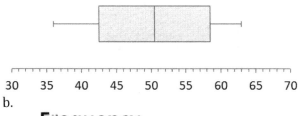

b.

Frequency

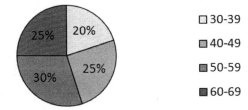

- ☐ 30-39
- ▨ 40-49
- ▧ 50-59
- ▣ 60-69

c.

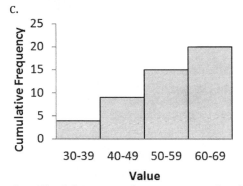

d.   All of these graphs represent the data set.

Science

67. Which of the following statements correctly compares rocks and minerals?

a.   Minerals may contain traces of organic compounds, while rocks do not.

b.   Rocks are classified by their formation and the minerals they contain, while minerals are classified by their chemical composition and physical properties.

c.   Both rocks and minerals can be polymorphs.

d.   Both rocks and minerals may contain mineraloids.

68. Fossils are least likely to be found in

a. sedimentary rock.
b. metamorphic rock.
c. igneous rock.
d. Fossils are commonly found in all types of rock.

69. Which of the following is never true of a chemical reaction?

a. Matter is neither gained nor lost.
b. Heat is absorbed or released.
c. The rate of the reaction increases with temperature.
d. There are a different number of atoms for the products and the reactants.

70. The following represents a simple food chain. What trophic level contains the greatest amount of energy?

$$\text{tree} \rightarrow \text{caterpillar} \rightarrow \text{frog} \rightarrow \text{snake} \rightarrow \text{hawk} \rightarrow \text{worm}$$

a. tree
b. caterpillar
c. hawk
d. worm

71. Tropical climate zones are characterized by:

a. Extreme temperature variations between night and day.
b. Extreme temperature variations between seasons.
c. Frequent rainfall.
d. Relatively constant, cold temperatures (35°F - 45°F)

72. Which of the following is an example of chemical weathering?

a. Rain freezing on the roadway
b. Ivy growing on the side of a wooden house
c. Vinegar fizzing when poured on a rock
d. A river carrying sediment downstream

73. What happens to the temperature of a substance as it is changing phase from a liquid to a solid?

a. Its temperature increases due to the absorption of latent heat.
b. Its temperature decreases due to the heat of vaporization.
c. Its temperature decreases due to the latent heat of fusion.
d. Its temperature remains the same due to the latent heat of fusion.

74. Which action will help dissolve a gas in a liquid if the gas and liquid are placed in a sealed container?

a. Heat the liquid.
b. Cool the liquid.
c. Shake the container.
d. Decrease the pressure on the lid.

75. How are igneous rocks formed?

    a. Years of sediment are laid down on top of each other and forced together

    b. Acid rain caused by pollution creates holes in metamorphic rocks

    c. Dust and pebbles are pressed together underground from Earth's heat and pressure

    d. Magma from a volcanic eruption cools and hardens

76. What type of compound is formed by the combination of two or more non-metallic elements with one another?

    a. Organic

    b. Ionic

    c. Covalent

    d. Chemical

77. Which of the following is an example of a descriptive study?

    a. correlational studies of populations

    b. identifying a control

    c. statistical data analysis

    d. identifying dependent and independent variables

78. Which of the following represents a chemical change?

    a. Sublimation of water

    b. A spoiling apple

    c. Dissolution of salt in water

    d. Breaking a rock in half

79. What happens to gas particles as temperature increases?

    a. The average kinetic energy decreases while the intermolecular forces increase.

    b. The average kinetic energy increases while the intermolecular forces decrease.

    c. Both the average kinetic energy and the intermolecular forces decrease.

    d. Both the average kinetic energy and the intermolecular forces increase.

80. To teach early physics concepts, an EC teacher gives students an activity of rolling balls down ramps. The teacher asks them questions like what would happen if one ramp were longer or higher; if two different sizes of ramps were used; if they started two balls rolling down a ramp at the same time, etc. Which skills in the scientific process do the children use during this activity?

    a. Observation and communication

    b. They use every one of these skills.

    c. Skills of inference and prediction

    d. Measurements and comparisons

81. Which of the following is correct regarding how objects produce sound and how we hear it?

    a. Sound is something that causes vibrations in the air.

    b. Sound waves are vibrations disturbing media like air.

    c. Sound causes vibrations in the air but not in the ear.

    d. Sound is the same energy type in the ear and brain.

82. The scientific method is a series of steps to ____.

    a. solve a problem
    b. gather information
    c. ask a scientific question
    d. formulate a hypothesis

83. The behaviors of living organisms are changed and shaped by:

    a. Primarily internal stimuli.
    b. Primarily external stimuli.
    c. Preset genetic programs.
    d. Internal and external cues.

Social Studies

84. According to family systems theory, which family system component reflects the family's physical and emotional environment and its emotional quality?

    a. Hierarchy
    b. Boundaries
    c. Climate
    d. Equilibrium

85. The Tropic of Capricorn:

    a. separates the northern and southern hemispheres.
    b. separates the eastern and western hemispheres.
    c. is the southernmost latitude at which the sun can appear directly overhead at noon.
    d. is the northernmost latitude at which the sun can appear directly overhead at noon.

86. Most federal judges have served as local judges, lawyers, and law professors. These are _____ qualifications.

    a. Formal
    b. Required
    c. Informal
    d. Recommended

87. In developing self-awareness, which of these can infants take relatively the longest to achieve?

    a. Showing eye-hand coordination by systematically reaching for and touching things
    b. Telling apart video of themselves from video of others doing the exact same things
    c. Using their sitting, posture, and balance levels to regulate their reaching for things
    d. Telling videos of them apart from video of other babies dressed in the same things

88. An adult places a sticker on a small child's face and then introduces a mirror. When the child sees the sticker in the mirror, s/he reaches toward her/his face to remove it rather than toward the mirror. Which level of self-awareness does this demonstrate?

    a. Permanence
    b. Differentiation
    c. Situation
    d. Identification

89. On which of the following maps would the scale be largest?

    a. A map of Benelux nations
    b. A map of Senegal
    c. A map of Rio de Janeiro
    d. A map of Greenwich Village

90. Which of the following is a possible absolute location for New Orleans?

    a. 30° S, 90° E
    b. 30° N, 90° E
    c. 30° S, 90° W
    d. 30° N, 90° W

91. Which of the following is *not* a method of representing relief on a physical map?

    a. Symbols
    b. Color
    c. Shading
    d. Contour Lines

92. Which of the following are more appreciated by individualistic cultures than by collectivist cultures?

    a. Socially and relationally oriented behaviors
    b. Working together for the good of the group
    c. Interdependence rather than independence
    d. Scientific thinking and manipulation of objects

93. Regarding cultural influences on parental childcare and education preferences, which result is true?

    a. Hispanic families in the U.S. are found to use preschool centers more.
    b. Hispanic families in the U.S. are found to prefer home/family settings.
    c. Caucasian and Hispanic families in the U.S. use center and home care equally.
    d. Caucasian families in the U.S. are likely to prefer family/home settings.

94. Which statement is most accurate regarding how educators in America can work with parents who are immigrants to this country?

    a. Where parents and educators disagree on educational goals, educators must convince these parents to agree with them.
    b. When children have developmental/learning problems, parents may need educators to inform them of available services.
    c. When parents from other cultures do not advocate for their children to get needed services, this is due to a lack of interest.
    d. When immigrant parents do not advocate for their children to get needed services, they are resisting confronting problems.

95. According to research into differences among culturally diverse parents in America's age expectations for EC developmental milestones, which of the following is correct?

a. Assessment data are no more likely to be misinterpreted when educators and parents have different rather than the same cultures.
b. Due to cultural variations in when children achieve milestones, educators need not worry about developmental assessments.
c. What parents from one culture view as developmentally normal can indicate developmental delay to parents from another culture.
d. Regardless of parental cultural background, not reaching a developmental milestone by a certain age is always a cause for concern.

96. In geography, which of the following is the best example of the concept of area differentiation?

a. Fishermen find more use in the ocean than farmers; naturalists use forests more than academics.
b. A region where farming is the main pursuit is rural; one where manufacturing dominates is urban.
c. Land that is settled first or most frequently is often near natural resources like water, forests, etc.
d. In one village, the predominant occupation is farming; in another village, fishing is more prevalent.

97. The physical geography of a region most directly affects which of the following?

a. The religious beliefs of the native population
b. The family structure of the native population
c. The dietary preferences of the native population
d. The language spoken by the native population

98. In which environment would you most likely find animals that estivate, or sleep during the day?

a. Desert
b. Temperate forest
c. Tundra
d. Grasslands

99. Which of the following is accurate regarding chronological thinking in studying history?

a. Middle school students should be able to analyze patterns of historical succession.
b. Chronological thinking is necessary to see cause-and-effect relationships in history.
c. Students should not be expected to interpret data from timelines until high school.
d. Teachers should avoid using narratives to instruct younger students in chronology.

100. Of the following, which applies to EC activities that can help teach civics?

a. Children's literature promotes literacy rather than applying to civics concepts.
b. Situations in stories make civics concepts more real and concrete for children.
c. Young children identify with characters in stories, distracting them from civics.
d. Writing and revising class rules in small groups will not teach any civics ideas.

Arts

101. Which of the following activities would be most appropriate for helping students develop an appreciation for the value and role of art in U.S. society?

a. Having students create a slide show presentation about a famous American artist
b. Asking students to create a timeline showing when famous works of American art were created
c. Taking students on a field trip to an art museum
d. Asking students to write an essay comparing and contrasting the influence that two famous American artists or artworks had on U.S. society

102. Which element of art will give preschoolers the most tactile aesthetic experience?

a. Line
b. Color
c. Shape
d. Texture

103. What is NOT true of aesthetic experiences for preschoolers with the element of line in visual art?

a. They are a good way to help children extend symbol recognition.
b. They can help develop young children's ability for comparison.
c. They use the best element for instructing children in 3-D shapes.
d. They can be used to give children experiences with various tools.

104. In music, the frequencies of individual sound waves equate to:

a. Pitch.
b. Tempo.
c. Rhythm.
d. Harmony.

105. What do EC aesthetic learning activities focusing on shape accomplish for preschoolers?

a. They develop concept-forming abilities but do not teach any math skills.
b. They develop creativity and imagination as well as early geometry skills.
c. They develop children's early math skills without using creative thinking.
d. They develop skills to identify differences rather than to form concepts.

106. Ms. Franklin is teaching a second-grade class a lesson on ceramics. The most appropriate activity for students at this grade level would be:

a. making pinch pots and coil pots.
b. throwing pots using a pottery wheel.
c. making and attaching handles to pots.
d. glazing pots using a kiln.

107. Which of the following is accurate regarding shape, form, and value in visual art?

a. Shapes in art are always positive and defined by outlines.
b. Biomorphic shapes in art are shapes which are geometric.
c. Value in visual works of art is dependent upon the colors.
d. Form has mass in 3-D art but appears to have it in 2-D art.

108. Which of the following best applies to EC aesthetic experiences with the element of color?

a. EC teachers should demonstrate mixing paint colors before having children do this.
b. EC teachers should not involve other modalities such as songs or stories with color.
c. EC teachers should present color samples to children rather than artists' paintings.
d. EC teachers should teach color names, not discrimination or classification abilities.

109. Which of these is an example of art produced to serve a physical purpose?

a. Depression photography the FSA commissioned
b. The "Last Supper" painting by Leonardo Da Vinci
c. Raku pottery bowls for Japanese tea ceremonies
d. Some of the satirical artworks of Francisco Goya

110. Among the artistic processes of creating, performing, and responding, in which order do these steps of the creating process occur?

a. Imagining; planning; evaluating and refining; presenting
b. Planning; imagining; presenting; evaluating and refining
c. Evaluating and refining; planning; presenting; imagining
d. Presenting; imagining; evaluating and refining; planning

Health and Physical Education

111. Which of these is most accurate about opportunities that physical activity provides?

a. Children develop self-efficacy as well as self-esteem through effort and perseverance.
b. Children develop their language skills younger than motor skills to express themselves.
c. Children develop physical skills through games and sports but do not learn social skills.
d. Children enjoy interacting socially in games but do not naturally seek physical activity.

112. During which age range do children's motor skills normally develop the fastest?

a. Birth to four years
b. From one to five years
c. From three to seven years
d. From two to six years

113. The World Health Organization recommends that between the ages of five and seventeen, children should do which of the following in terms of physical activity?

a. At least three weekly sessions of aerobic activity and one hour daily of weight-bearing activity
b. At least one hour of daily aerobic activity and three weekly sessions of weight-bearing activity
c. At least three days a week for aerobic activity and three days a week of weight-bearing activity
d. At least one hour a day for aerobic activity and one hour per day for weight-bearing activity

114. What is correct regarding the standards for physical education set forth by the National Association for Sport and Physical Education (NASPE)?
   a. Their criteria for physical fitness do not directly mention health.
   b. They mention social interaction but not self-respect as a benefit.
   c. These standards do not address diet as a part of physical fitness.
   d. They assume exercise confers pleasure and so do not mention it.

115. What have some researchers found about physical exercise relative to school performance?
   a. Children who sit more can focus attention better than those who are more active.
   b. Children who are more physically active do better on standardized academic tests.
   c. Children who study more have better working memory than more active children.
   d. Children who exercise more do not show as good problem-solving skills as others.

116. What percentage of total calorie consumption should be from fat?
   a. 10–35 percent
   b. 20–35 percent
   c. 10–25 percent
   d. 20–30 percent

117. Which of the following best describes eccentric movement?
   a. Jogging uphill
   b. Walking down stairs
   c. Doing a sit up
   d. Throwing a ball

118. Cardiac output is the product of what two factors?
   a. Heart rate and stroke volume
   b. Stroke volume and blood pressure
   c. Heart rate and pulse
   d. Stroke volume and oxygen consumption

119. Which of the following is an example of how emotional/behavioral factors can affect young children's levels of physical activity and fitness?
   a. A child diagnosed with ADHD is physically so overactive that he becomes exhausted.
   b. A child diagnosed with asthma needs monitoring for breathing problems in exercise.
   c. A child diagnosed with diabetes needs exercise watched and coordinated with diet.
   d. A child diagnosed with disabilities needs adaptive equipment for physical activities.

120. Which of the following best describes the purpose of rhythmic activities?
   a. To learn music tempo
   b. To learn how to perform
   c. To learn how to control the body
   d. To learn the locomotor movements

Answer Key and Explanations #2

Language Arts

1. A: The pragmatic component of oral language development involves learning the rules for using speech that is appropriate to various social situations, including how to speak and when to speak or not speak. The phonological component (B) of oral language development involves learning the rules for putting speech sounds or phonemes into words. The semantic component (C) of oral language development involves learning the rules for combining morphemes into words (e.g., "book" + "s" = "books") and words into sentences to convey the meanings intended. The syntactic component (D) of oral language development involves learning the rules for combining words in the correct sequence or order to create understandable sentences.

2. B: The teacher should group English language learner (ELL) and native English-speaking students heterogeneously to give ELL students authentic opportunities to use English to communicate regarding academic content with both native and non-native English speakers. They should not be grouped homogeneously (A) as this will restrict their academic English communication to being only with other non-native English speakers. In some cases it may be reassuring and supportive to place at least two ELLs per heterogeneous group (C), but this is not always necessary and, in some classes, can be impossible depending on numbers of students. As heterogeneous grouping will give ELLs opportunities to communicate with both native and non-native English speakers and homogeneous grouping will not, it is incorrect that the grouping will make no difference (D).

3. A: One teaching technique that is effective for promoting print awareness in young children is to have them narrate books that contain only pictures. This is even more effective when teachers reinforce the activity by providing a directly related reward, such as having them eat pancakes after they narrate the picture book *Pancakes*. Even with young children who cannot read yet, it is good to read to them from large-print books (B) that they can more easily view, facilitating their beginning to learn to read sooner. Teachers should label objects and areas in their classrooms using both pictures and words together (C) to teach and reinforce correspondences between spoken and written words. Storybooks teachers read to preschoolers should use predictable, familiar words (D).

4. C: Among categories of phonological awareness activities, working with rhymes is less difficult than others. Within the rhyming category, the easiest activity for children is to identify which words they hear rhyme with each other. The second easiest rhyme activity is being able to discriminate rhyming from non-rhyming words by picking which words in a list rhyme (B). The hardest rhyme activity is creating rhymes by naming words that rhyme with a word that is given (A). Therefore, these are not all equally difficult (D).

5. D: None; sight words cannot be decoded. Readers must learn to recognize these words as wholes on sight. Sight words have irregular spelling. Segmenting them into syllables or using a phonemic approach are ineffective strategies to aid a reader in recognizing a sight word because these approaches depend on rules a sight word doesn't follow. Word families group words that share common patterns of consonants and vowels. The spelling of those words is, therefore, regular because they follow a predictable pattern. Sight words are irregular and do not follow a predictable pattern and must be instantaneously recognized for writing fluency. No decoding is useful.

6. A: When a child's reading out loud sounds choppy and awkward, this is a sign that the child lacks reading fluency. To read fluently, children must not only sound fluent when reading aloud (B), but also read quickly, smoothly, and effortlessly when reading silently to achieve good comprehension and time-efficiency. When reading aloud, fluent readers not only read the words accurately, but also supply the appropriate expression (C) for the meanings in the text. Reading fluency is measured by *both* speed *and* accuracy (D) in reading.

7. B: If students read two versions of the same fairy tale narrated by two different characters, they can contrast the versions of events that are described and discuss how each character's situations and feelings may affect the way the story is told. Choice A and choice C allow students to respond individually to the story, but they do not offer students the opportunity to compare situations from two different points of view. Choice D helps students compare and contrast two sets of events, but it also does not address two different points of view.

8. A: Venn diagrams consist of overlapping circles, which visually represent the similarities and differences between two or more items. They are commonly used for compare and contrast activities. Story maps are used to identify the components of fictional stories, such as the characters and setting. Five W's charts are used to identify details in stories by answering who, what, where, when, and why questions. T-charts allow students to contrast two items, but there is no visual representation of the similarities between them.

9. C: Text features are one factor used to level books. They help determine how much support readers have in decoding and comprehending the text. For example, pictures are one text feature essential for early readers. Other text features, such as headings and labels, can assist readers with expository texts. Therefore, text features are considered when leveling books. Considering both the author's purpose and craft can help students comprehend texts, but they do not typically affect leveling. Interest level will vary from student to student and is also not typically considered when leveling books.

10. D: Children go through five identified stages in writing development. Scribbling and drawing (A) is the first stage, when children explore line, form, and space as they hold crayons, etc., in their little fists. The second stage, letter-like forms and shapes (D), is when they first realize that meanings are represented through written symbols. Their drawings and "writings" now include circles, squares, and other shapes, randomly placed with minimal spatial orientation. It is common in this stage for children to write figures and then ask their parents what they "say." In the third stage (B), children start to write real letters. They usually produce written consonants first, without awareness of letter-to-sound correspondence; they develop this gradually. They enjoy writing their own name initials. In the fourth, letters and spaces stage (C), children understand the concept of words, space words correctly, and use 1:1 word correspondence. They can write initial and final word phonemes, and experiment with constructing and punctuating sentences. The fifth stage is conventional writing and spelling.

11. C: The goal of a persuasive essay is to convince the reader that the author's position or opinion on a controversial topic is correct. That opinion or position is called the argument. A persuasive essay argues a series of points, supported by facts and evidence.

12. B: Typically, after students write something, their teachers may ask them to reflect upon what they wrote, which would mean that this is NOT a prewriting activity. In writing exercises, teachers will typically ask students to plan (A) what they will write in order to clearly define their main topic and organize their work. Many teachers find it helps students to visualize (C) what they are reading and/or want to write about and make drawings of what they visualize as preparation for writing.

Brainstorming (D) is another common prewriting activity designed to generate multiple ideas from which students can then select to include in their writing.

13. D: Knowing your purpose for writing means knowing what you want to achieve with the content of your writing, and knowing this will determine your writing style. Your choice of words and how formal or informal your writing is—your diction—*does* affect your style (A). Diction and tone should be consistent in your writing style, and should reflect vocabulary and writing patterns that suit your writing purpose best. Style is not added later to give writing personality (B). It develops from your purpose for writing, or what you want to accomplish with your writing. Style *is* directly related to your control of the content (C) of your writing.

14. C: There is currently a wide variety of technology resources available that can support class instruction. However, teachers must choose carefully in order to ensure that the technology is useful and relevant to his or her intended learning outcomes for the class. The language lab described allows students to experience text through listening *and* reading, thereby utilizing different processes in the brain. The interactive modules also support decoding and comprehension skills that go along with the texts. This use of technology reinforces important skills in a way that will be unique and interesting for the students.

15. C: Once the students' notecards have been checked and edited for accuracy, they can easily be used to demonstrate the process of organizing ideas in an essay or research paper. Students can use their notecards as aids for making their outlines. They simply have to arrange the notecards in an appropriate order and add pertinent information to bridge the ideas together in their writing.

16. D: For clarity in a written speech, the speechwriter must define the purpose of the speech in advance (a). For audiences to follow it, the speech must be organized logically (b). Making an outline first gives the speechwriter a blueprint to focus and direct the speech to accomplish its purpose (c). Good sentence construction and precise word choice are equally important in speeches as in reading text (d).

17. B: Spelling is often taught in a systematic way. Students receive words and memorize them for quizzes and tests. However, spelling is related to many aspects of language and must be treated as a dynamic subject. Integrating the words into other parts of language instruction will help students not only learn how to spell correctly, but also to recall meanings of words and various rules of English spelling and grammar. By using the same words in different subjects, the students will retain the information more readily than if they study the words intensely for one week in only one context.

18. B: This sentence correctly capitalizes the place name of Washington, D.C., a proper noun. The word "president" is incorrectly capitalized in (A): it should only be capitalized when used as a proper noun, e.g., "President Obama." But when a civil title is used instead of a name as it is here, it is not capitalized. The word "south" is incorrectly capitalized in (C). Compass directions are not capitalized, as in "coming south" or "going south." They are capitalized only when referring to actual regions, as in "We live in the South." The words "science" and "math" are incorrectly capitalized in (D). Academic subjects are not capitalized. It is correct to capitalize "English" because it is derived from the proper noun "England." *Specific* titles of classes or courses, like "Elementary Algebra" or "Math 101" should be capitalized, but general nouns like "science" and "math" should not.

19. B: In this example, the reader uses the context of the sentence to understand the meaning of "reeds" rather than "reads" without needing to know how each is spelled, because the former makes sense in the context while the latter does not, semantically or grammatically. The reader is not using phonics (A) because both words sound the same, and in this case both "ea" and "ee" have the same sound. The reader is not using spelling (C) because the question states that s/he is unfamiliar with seeing these words in print. The reader cannot be assumed to be using pictures (D) in this case because the question never states there are any illustrations of the text.

20. A: An idiom is a type of figurative language in which the entire phrase has a unique meaning that cannot be determined from the meanings of the individual words. This idiom means that it is raining very hard, which does not match the literal meaning of the phrase. Proverbs are short, well-known sayings that offer wisdom or advice. A simile is a figure of speech used to compare two things using *like* or *as*. A metaphor is a figure of speech used to compare two things without the use of *like* or *as*.

21. C: Tier-two words. Tier-two words are words that are used with high frequency across a variety of disciplines or words with multiple meanings. They are characteristic of mature language users. Knowing these words is crucial to attaining an acceptable level of reading comprehension and communication skills.

22. B: When students learn to summarize text, they learn to identify the most important ideas in a text AND organize those ideas in their minds (a); identify the themes, problems, and solutions in the text (b); monitor reading comprehension; AND correctly sequence (c) story events, essay points, etc. Graphic organizers, drawing, and other visuals help students visualize connections more than summarizing (d), a more mental and verbal than visual activity (though such visualization can aid summarization).

23. D: Comparison-contrast (a) paragraph structural patterns identify similarities and differences between two or more things. Cause-and-effect (b) patterns identify causes of some occurrence or characteristic, or effects of some causal factors. They may move from cause to effect or from effect to cause, but otherwise do not sequence any series of events chronologically. Analogies (c) compare two things from different categories or are otherwise not usually compared. Process (d) patterns describe or explain some progression, most often in chronological sequence.

24. D: When students are unfamiliar with group discussions, teachers should not introduce these by beginning with topics below student age level (a); such topics will bore students and fail to engage them. Neither should teachers assign group discussion topics above student age levels (b), which will confuse, lose, and/or overwhelm them. They should take student cognitive, emotional, behavioral, and social levels of development into account when choosing discussion topics. For all students, and especially those inexperienced with discussion groups, teachers should explain *and* model appropriate behaviors—not just explain (c)—before beginning a discussion. These behaviors include eye contact and confirming and restating others' messages.

25. D: Emergent literacy theory incorporates influences from Piaget and Vygotsky, who both described reading and writing as developmental processes that go through successive, discrete stages. Emergent literacy theorists have done extensive research and found that when young children "reread" storybooks, this does not mean they have memorized them (A) but rather that they are reconstructing the books' meanings. Research also finds that young children's invented spellings do afford information about their familiarity with specific phonetic components of words (B). Emergent literacy theorists find it crucial for adults to read to young children regardless of how young they are (C).

26. A: It is a standard of Information Literacy (IL) that students must use their own critical thinking skills to evaluate the quality of the information and its sources before they use it. Another standard is that the student should ascertain how much information s/he needs for his/her purposes first; deciding this after uncovering excessive information is inefficient (B). An additional IL standard is to access necessary information in an efficient and effective way. However, none of these standards include the idea that students will lose incidental learning or broadness of scope by doing so (C). IL standards include the principle that students *should* use the information they find in ways that are effective for attaining their specific purposes (D).

27. A: During interactive writing experiences, teachers and students work together to create writing pieces. Teachers and students share the writing utensils, with teachers guiding the students as they record their thoughts. In shared writing experiences, teachers record students' thoughts on paper. Students do not help with the writing. In independent writing, students utilize the strategies they have learned to complete writing pieces independently. Guided writing occurs when teachers work with small groups of strategically grouped students on targeted writing skills.

28. A: The /p/ sound is among the earliest phonemes to develop, from ages 1.5 to 3 years old. The /ʒ/ phoneme (B) has the oldest age norm for normal development—5.5 years to 8.5 years old is a typical range for children to acquire correct production of this sound. The /v/ sound (C) typically develops in most children from the ages of 4 to 8 years. Most children develop correct articulation of the /s/ sound (D) by 2.5 to 4 years old. Hence, not all kindergarteners, who are typically around 5 years old, are expected to master phonemes with acquisition norm ranges older than 5-8 years. A 5-year-old is *most* likely to be referred for SLP evaluation if s/he does not correctly produce /p/, which children normally develop by around 3 years old.

29. C: ESL students can understand the teacher's questions, as well as engage in informal conversations with peers and adults, using conversational English. However, in order to understand their school textbooks (A), solve mathematical word problems (B), and understand and communicate novel and/or abstract concepts (D) as well as write papers and reports, they must master academic English, which is more difficult.

30. D: The alphabetic principle is the concept that printed letters and letter combinations correspond to speech sounds. In order to learn the sounds that alphabet letters represent, children must first know the names of the letters. First they learn letter names, then they learn the shapes of the letters (A), and then they learn the sounds indicated by the letters (B). They learn each of these in sequence rather than all at the same time (C).

31. B: Indirect ways in which students receive instruction and learn vocabulary include through daily conversations, reading on their own, and being read aloud to by adults. Direct instruction and learning in vocabulary include teachers' providing extended instruction exposing students repeatedly to vocabulary words in multiple teaching contexts, teachers' pre-teaching specific words found in text prior to students' reading it, and teachers' instructing students over extended time periods and having them actively work with vocabulary words.

32. B: Prior knowledge is knowledge the student brings from previous life or learning experiences to the act of reading. It is not possible for a student to fully comprehend new knowledge without first integrating it with prior knowledge. Prior knowledge, which rises from experience and previous learning, provides a framework by which new knowledge gained from the act of reading can be integrated. Every act of reading enriches a student's well of prior knowledge and increases that student's future ability to comprehend more fully any new knowledge acquired through reading.

33. A: Teachers should introduce high-utility letters/sounds, i.e. those used most frequently in words, like a, s, h, and m, first to young children. Letters/sounds like *x* as in *box*, *gh* as in *through*, and *ey* as in *they* are of lower, not high (B) utility; hence they have lower priority and can be taught later. Young children can more easily produce continuous consonant sounds like f, m, n, r, and s, so teachers should start with these. Children are more likely to distort stopped consonants like p, b, t, d, k, and g, which should be taught after the continuous consonants (C). While there is no exact set rate for teaching phonics because of individual differences among children, a reasonable rate is about 2-4 sound-letter relationships per week; 10-15 a week (D) are far too many for most young children.

34. D: Dog, sit, leg. CVC words are composed of a consonant, a vowel, and a consonant. To learn to read them, students must be familiar with the letters used and their sounds. A teacher can present a word like *sit* to students who also know the consonants *b/f/h/p* and ask them to create a word family of other CVC words. The students will be able to read *bit, fit, hit,* and *pit* because they are similar to the word *sit* they have just learned.

35. C: Cause–effect words. Signal words give the reader hints about the purpose of a particular passage. Some signal words are concerned with comparing/contrasting, some with cause and effect, some with temporal sequencing, some with physical location, and some with a problem and its solution. The words *since, whether,* and *accordingly* are words used when describing an outcome. Outcomes have causes.

36. D: This is an example of a compound-complex sentence. A simple sentence contains a subject and a verb and expresses a complete thought. Its subject and/or verb may be compound (e.g., "John and Mary" as subject and "comes and goes" as verb). A complex sentence contains an independent clause and one or more dependent clauses. The independent and dependent clause(s) are joined by a subordinating conjunction or a relative pronoun. A compound sentence contains two independent clauses—two simple sentences—connected by a coordinating conjunction. A compound-complex (also called complex-compound) sentence, as its name implies, combines both compound and complex sentences: it combines more than one independent clause with at least one dependent clause. In the example sentence given, the first two clauses, joined by "however," are independent, and the clause modifying "actual test questions," beginning with "which cover," is a relative, dependent clause.

Mathematics

37. B: To help children learn to apply formal math to solving real-life, everyday problems, teachers need to establish connections between the intuitive mathematical thinking that preschool children naturally use. To do this, they should *not* emphasize a view of math as a group of rules and procedures (A): this is how children beginning school often come to view formal math, and it *prevents* them from realizing they can apply it to real life for solving problems. Teachers can, however, help children see connections between their natural problem-solving mathematical processes and the math they are learning in school, by providing concrete objects familiar to children that they can manipulate to work through math problems (C), because young children think concretely, and using concrete manipulatives helps them understand abstract concepts and prepares them for progressing to abstract thought. Teachers can also illustrate math concepts using real-life examples relevant to children's real-life experiences (D), and describe children's activities using math vocabulary words, allowing children to realize how they naturally use mathematical operations (D).

38. C: Children develop symbolic representation early, as when they play creating "make-believe"/"pretend" scenarios. Counting on their fingers (B) is another early example of emerging math skills. Once they can control writing implements beyond scribbling, they may keep counts of things or events by make written tallies using tick-marks (D), check-marks, and even words once they are able to write these. Young children will also represent things by drawing pictures of them, and drawing simple maps (A) of places and/or directions—involving real-life locations and also make-believe ones, as with "pirate" treasure maps. Children will progress to making graphs (C) to depict numbers of things/people/events, intervals of time, and relationships, when they are older.

39. C: The midpoint may be calculated by using the formula $m = \left(\frac{x_1+x_2}{2}, \frac{y_1+y_2}{2}\right)$. Thus, the midpoint of the line segment shown may be written as $m = \left(\frac{1+8}{2}, \frac{2+8}{2}\right)$, which simplifies to $m = (4.5, 5)$.

40. D: The perimeter of the triangle is equal to the sum of the side lengths. The length of the longer diagonal side may be represented as $d = \sqrt{(4-1)^2 + (5-2)^2}$, which simplifies to $d = \sqrt{18}$. The length of the shorter diagonal side may be represented as $d = \sqrt{(6-4)^2 + (2-5)^2}$, which simplifies to $d = \sqrt{13}$. The base length is 5 units. Thus, the perimeter is equal to $5 + \sqrt{18} + \sqrt{13}$, which is approximately 12.85 units. Since each unit represents 5 miles, the total distance she will have walked is equal to the product of 12.85 and 5, or approximately 64 miles.

41. A: It is true that manipulative objects have been found so effective for young children's learning that Horizons and other early math curricula actually require their use. Manipulatives that children can see, feel, and work with not only help young children who learn best through visual, tactile, and kinesthetic modalities, but they also help other young children (B) because young children's learning is mainly via looking at, touching, holding, arranging, and moving concrete things as well as being fun (D). Young children mostly do not understand abstract concepts yet, and are even less likely to understand them when presented in abstract form, but they are more able to access some abstract ideas that are presented in concrete forms (C).

42. C: The expression representing the monthly charge for Company A is $\$25 + \$0.05m$, where m is the time in minutes spent talking on the phone. Set this expression equal to the monthly charge for Company B, which is $50. Solve for m to find the number of minutes for which the two companies charge the same amount:

$$\$25 + \$0.05m = \$50$$
$$\$0.05m = \$25$$
$$m = 500$$

Notice that the answer choices are given in hours, not in minutes. Since there are 60 minutes in an hour, $m = \frac{500}{60}$ hours $= 8\frac{1}{3}$ hours. One-third of an hour is twenty minutes, so m = 8 hours, 20 minutes.

43. C: A system of linear equations can be solved by using matrices or by using the graphing, substitution, or elimination (also called linear combination) method. The elimination method is shown here:

$$3x + 4y = 2$$
$$2x + 6y = -2$$

In order to eliminate x by linear combination, multiply the top equation by 2 and the bottom equation by –3 so that the coefficients of the x-terms will be additive inverses.

$$2(3x + 4y = 2)$$
$$-3(2x + 6y = -2)$$

Then, add the two equations and solve for y.

$$6x + 8y = 4$$
$$\underline{-6x - 18y = 6}$$
$$-10y = 10$$
$$y = -1$$

Substitute -1 for y in either of the given equations and solve for x.

$$3x + 4(-1) = 2$$
$$3x - 4 = 2$$
$$3x = 6$$
$$x = 2$$

The solution to the system of equations is $(2, -1)$.

44. D: The cross-section is a hexagon.

45. B: One way that teachers can help young children connect mathematics to real everyday life is to describe children's typical activities to them using mathematical vocabulary words. This enables children to realize how they routinely perform mathematical operations every day. Formal math instruction (A) too often results in young children's view of math as an isolated set of rules that they do not apply for problem-solving in their everyday lives. Teachers can bridge formal and intuitive mathematics by using manipulatives in math that are familiar to children rather than novel (C). Familiar objects help children relate math to life. Similarly, when teachers introduce children to new math concepts, illustrating them using examples related to children's real-life experiences rather than original but unfamiliar examples (D) will make the concepts more relevant to them personally—and thereby more understandable as well as more meaningful.

46. C: The amount he donates is equal to $0.01(45,000)$. Thus, he donates $450.

47. D: This situation may be modeled by an arithmetic sequence, with a common difference of 4 and an initial value of 3. Substituting the common difference and initial value into the formula, $a_n = a_1 + (n - 1)d$, gives $a_n = 3 + (n - 1)4$, which simplifies to $a_n = 4n - 1$.

48. B: The following proportion may be written and solved for x: $\frac{15}{5} = \frac{6}{x}$. Cross multiplying results in $15x = 30$. Dividing by 15 gives $x = 2$. Thus, the shadow cast by the man is 2 feet in length.

49. C: To figure out how many times a specific event should occur, multiply the theoretical probability by the total number of events. The theoretical probability of a coin toss resulting in heads is 1/2. Multiply 1/2 by 300 to get an expected value of 150 coin tosses resulting in heads.

50. B: Since Mr. Mancelli has eight candy bars, he can make at most eight identical bags, each containing a single candy bar and a single package of gum; in this case, however, he will have four packages of gum remaining. To determine the greatest number of prize bags he can make so that no candy bars or packages of gum remain, he needs to find the greatest common divisor (or greatest common factor) of 8 and 12. Factors of 8 include 1, 2, 4, and 8. Factors of 12 include 1, 2, 3, 4, 6, and 12. The greatest common divisor of 8 and 12 is 4. He can make four prize bags, each of which contains two candy bars and three packages of gum.

51. C: Addition and subtraction of whole numbers up to 20 using concrete and pictorial models and number sentences is the appropriate level for first-grade students. Numbers up to 1000 and number pairs are appropriate for third-grade students. Counting by ones and tens is appropriate for kindergarten.

52. A: A hexagon has six sides. A hexagonal prism has 8 faces consisting of two hexagonal bases and six rectangular lateral faces. This results in 18 edges and 12 vertices. Therefore, the correct choice is A.

53. D: The theoretical probability of tossing any particular number is $\frac{1}{6}$. Since she tosses a two $\frac{3}{12}$, or $\frac{1}{4}$, times, the experimental probability of tossing a 2 is greater than the theoretical probability. The experimental probability should grow closer to the experimental probability as she tosses the die more times.

54. C: Substitute 2 for each x-value and simplify: $f(2) = \frac{2^3 - 2(2) + 1}{3(2)} = \frac{8 - 4 + 1}{6} = \frac{5}{6}$

55. C: If l and w represent the length and width of the enclosed area, its perimeter is equal to $2l + 2w$; since the fence is positioned x feet from the lot's edges on each side, the perimeter of the lot is $2(l + 2x) + 2(w + 2x)$. Since the amount of money saved by fencing the smaller area is $432, and since the fencing material costs $12 per linear foot, 36 fewer feet of material are used to fence around the playground than would have been used to fence around the lot. This can be expressed:

$$2(l + 2x) + 2(w + 2x) - (2l + 2w) = 36$$
$$2l + 4x + 2w + 4x - 2l - 2w = 36$$
$$8x = 36$$
$$x = 4.5 \text{ ft}$$

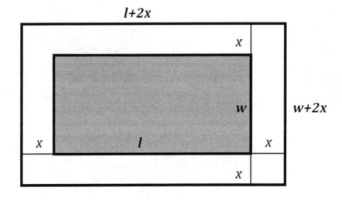

The difference in the area of the lot and the enclosed space is 141 yd^2, which is the same as 1,269 ft^2. So, $(l + 2x)(w + 2x) - lw = 1,269$. Substituting 4.5 for $l + w$,

$$(l + 9)(w + 9) - lw = 1,269$$
$$lw + 9l + 9w + 81 - lw = 1,269$$
$$9l + 9w = 1,188$$
$$9(l + w) = 1,188$$
$$l + w = 132 \text{ ft}$$

Therefore, the perimeter of the enclosed space, $2(l + w)$, is $2(132) = 264$ ft. The cost of 264 ft of fencing is $264 \times \$12 = \$3,168$.

56. D: When young children begin to play "make-believe" or "pretend," they are demonstrating that they have acquired representation skills, i.e., using one thing to stand for/represent another. This occurs at early ages; hence (A) is incorrect. More examples of how children use representation skills include counting on their fingers (B)—fingers are concrete objects they use to represent numbers; drawing pictures (C)—pictures are themselves symbolic representations of real objects and people; and making marks to keep tallies (D) or counts of objects, people, turns taken, game scores, etc.

57. D: Each of these choices is an example of how a different math process skill can be applied during children's typical preschool activities. With a child who is sorting toys by color, when the teacher describes this activity to the child as classification (A), the teacher is connecting the informal activity with an application of mathematical vocabulary. When the teacher asks the child to explain how s/he is dividing up the toys (B), this applies the process of communication in mathematics. When the teacher asks the child once s/he is done sorting what other ways s/he could sort them (C), this applies the mathematical process skill of problem-solving.

58. C: The line through the center of the box represents the median. The median test score for Classes 1 and 2 is 82.

59. A: Marcus needs \$325 for the new gaming system. If he earns \$6.50 an hour, the number of hours he needs to work can be determined by dividing \$325 by \$6.50 which is written as $\frac{325}{6.50} = x$. Multiplying both sides of the equation by 6.50 yields $6.50x = 325$.

60. A: The probability that the dart will land in the inner circle is equal to the ratio of the area of inner circle to the area of the outer circle, or $\frac{\pi 3^2}{\pi 6^2}$. This reduces to $\frac{1}{4}$.

61. D: As adults, we know that one cookie, whether whole or broken into two pieces, is the same amount. However, as Piaget showed, young children who have not yet developed the cognitive ability to perform (mathematical or logical) mental operations do not know this. They focus ("centrate") on one aspect, e.g., the number of pieces, and fail to "conserve" the idea of an amount despite its appearance, division, or arrangement. Knowing the concepts of having three toys (A), of representing a number of objects symbolically with the corresponding number of fingers (B), and of addition, e.g., 2 + 1 = 3 using concrete objects like cookies (C), are all better examples of a young child's using mathematical concepts.

62. A: When adults play mental math games with young children, like those involving story problems, experts advise that this not be a one-way process: the adult and child should take turns so the child views the game as fair and reciprocal. When it is the child's turn to pose the problem, the adult must try to solve it, even when the child uses invented numbers (e.g., "gazillion"). It is more important for adults to ask questions of children than to give them the answers (B). Math games with young children should be fun for them, rather than being strictly factual like math tests (C). Young children should NOT be given unknown variable/number games while still in early childhood (D), as these are usually too abstract for them to understand until they are about five to six years old.

63. C: Piaget identified very young children's thinking as "preoperational", i.e., not yet formal (A), logical (B), or using hypothetical or deductive (D) processes. Rather, he labeled their thinking as intuitive. Young children naturally learn to use intuitive mathematical thought as they encounter and learn to solve everyday problems in their real-life experiences. They typically only develop formal, logical, and deductive mathematical thinking via the maturation of middle childhood and several years of formal education.

64. B: The volume of a sphere may be calculated using the formula $V = \frac{4}{3}\pi r^3$, where r represents the radius. Substituting 3.5 for r gives $V = \frac{4}{3}\pi(3.5)^3$, which simplifies to $V \approx 179.6$ in^3.

65. A: The vertical line of symmetry is represented by an equation of the form $x = a$. The horizontal line of symmetry is represented by an equation of the form $y = a$. One line of symmetry occurs at $x = -4$. The other line of symmetry occurs at $y = 6$.

66. D: To draw a box-and-whisker plot from the data, find the median, quartiles, and upper and lower limits. The median is $\frac{50+51}{2} = 50.5$, the lower quartile is $\frac{22+23}{2} = 22.5$, and the upper quartile is $\frac{57+60}{2} = 58.5$. The box of the box-and-whisker plot goes through the quartiles, and a line through the box represents the median of the data. The whiskers extend from the box to the lower and upper limits, unless there are any outliers in the set. In this case, there are no outliers, so the box-and-whisker plot in choice A correctly represents the data set.

To draw a pie chart, find the percentage of data contained in each of the ranges shown. There are four out of twenty numbers between 30 and 39, inclusive, so the percentage shown in the pie chart for that range of data is $\frac{4}{20} \cdot 100\% = 20\%$; there are five values between 40 to 49, inclusive, so the percentage of data for that sector is $\frac{5}{20} \cdot 100\% = 25\%$; $\frac{6}{20} \cdot 100\% = 30\%$ of the data is within the range of 50-59, and $\frac{5}{20} \cdot 100\% = 25\%$ is within the range of 60-69. The pie chart shows the correct percentage of data in each category.

To draw a cumulative frequency histogram, find the cumulative frequency of the data.

Range	Frequency	Cumulative frequency
30-39	4	4
40-49	5	9
50-59	6	15
60-69	5	20

The histogram shows the correct cumulative frequencies. Therefore, all of the graphs represent the data set.

Science

67. B: It is true that rocks are classified by their formation and the minerals they contain, while minerals are classified by their chemical composition and physical properties. Choice A is incorrect because rocks may contain traces of organic compounds. Choices C and D are incorrect because only minerals can be polymorphs and only rocks contain mineraloids.

68. C: Igneous rock. Fossils are least likely to be found in igneous rock. Igneous rock is formed by extreme heat as magma escapes through the Earth's crust and cools. The remains of plants and animals in fossil form are not usually preserved under these conditions. Sedimentary rock is where the abundance of fossils are found. Sedimentary rock is formed more slowly and is very abundant. Since soft mud and silts compress into layers, organisms can also be deposited. Metamorphic rock is rock that has undergone change by heat and pressure. This usually destroys any fossils, but occasionally fossil remains are distorted and can be found in metamorphic rock.

69. D: There may be a different number of atoms for the products and the reactants. This is not true of a chemical reaction. Chemical equations must be balanced on each side of the reaction. Balancing means the total number of atoms stays the same, but their arrangement within specific reactants and products can change. The law of conservation of matter states that matter can never be created or destroyed. Heat may be absorbed or released in a reaction; these are classified as endothermic and exothermic reactions, respectively. The rate of the reaction increases with temperature for most reactions.

70. A: In the food chain of tree → caterpillar → frog → snake → hawk → worm, the tree is at the trophic level with the greatest amount of energy. Trophic level refers to the position of an organism in a food chain. Energy is lost according to the laws of thermodynamics as one moves up the food chain because it is converted to heat when consumers consume. Primary producers, such as autotrophs, are organisms who are at the base and capture solar energy. Primary consumers are herbivores that feed on the producers. Secondary consumers consume primary consumers and so on. Decomposers get their energy from the consumption of dead plants and animals.

71. C: Tropical climate zones are characterized by frequent rainfall, especially during the monsoon season, and by moderate temperatures that vary little from season to season or between night and day. Tropical zones do experience frequent rainfall, which leads to abundant vegetation.

72. C: Vinegar fizzing when poured on a rock is an example of chemical weathering. Mechanical and chemical weathering are processes that break down rocks. Mechanical weathering breaks down rocks physically but does not change their chemical composition. Frost and abrasion are examples.

Water, oxygen, carbon dioxide and living organisms can lead to the chemical weathering of rock. Vinegar is a weak acid and will undergo a chemical reaction, evidenced by fizzing, with the rock. Rain freezing on the roadway is an example of the phase change of water from a liquid to a solid and may lead to physical weathering. Ivy growing on the side of a wooden house is incorrect since the house is not a rock. A river carrying sediment downstream is an example of erosion.

73. D: Its temperature remains the same due to the latent heat of fusion. The temperature of a substance during the time of any phase change remains the same. In this case, the phase change was from liquid to solid, or freezing. Latent heat of fusion, in this case, is energy that is released from the substance as it reforms its solid form. This energy will be released and the liquid will turn to solid before the temperature of the substance will decrease further. If the substance were changing from solid to liquid, the heat of fusion would be the amount of heat required to break apart the attractions between the molecules in the solid form to change to the liquid form. The latent heat of fusion is exactly the same quantity of energy for a substance for either melting or freezing. Depending on the process, this amount of heat would either be absorbed by the substance (melting) or released (freezing).

74. B: Cool the liquid. If a gas and a liquid are placed in a sealed container, cooling the liquid will help dissolve the gas into the liquid. Gasses have higher solubility in liquids at lower temperatures. At higher temperatures, the gas molecules will have more kinetic energy and will have enough energy to overcome intermolecular interactions with the liquid solvent and leave the solution. This also explains why heating the liquid is incorrect. Shaking the container is also incorrect as this would give the gas energy to escape. Decreasing the pressure on the lid may or may not significantly affect the pressure inside the vessel depending on the nature of the vessel, but decreasing the pressure inside the vessel would decrease the solubility of the gas in the liquid.

75. D: Igneous rocks are formed when magma in Earth erupts through cracks in the crust where it cools creating a hard structure with many air pockets or holes.

76. C: Covalent. Covalent compounds are usually formed by the combination of two or more non-metallic elements with one another. In these compounds, atoms share electrons. Ionic compounds are most often formed between a metal and a non-metal. Organic compounds are covalent compounds which contain carbon and hydrogen atoms. "Chemical compounds" is a general term that can mean any type of compound, either ionic or covalent.

77. A: A correlational study of a population is an example of a descriptive study. Choices B and C are examples of the controlled experimentation type of scientific investigation. Choice D is an example of the comparative data analysis type of scientific investigation.

78. B: A spoiling apple. A spoiling apple is an example of a chemical change. During a chemical change, one substance is changed into another. Oxidation, a chemical change, occurs when an apple spoils. Sublimation of water refers to the conversion between the solid and the gaseous phases of matter, with no intermediate liquid stage. This is a phase change, not a chemical reaction. Dissolution of salt in water refers to a physical change since the salt and water can be separated again by evaporating the water, which is a physical change. Breaking a rock is an example of a physical change where the form has changed but not the substance itself.

79. B: Temperature is a measure of the kinetic energy of particles. As temperature increases the average kinetic energy also increases. As the gas particles move more rapidly, they occupy a larger volume. The increase in speed of the individual particles combined with the greater distance over which any intermolecular forces must act results in a decrease in the intermolecular forces.

80. B: The activity described uses each of these skills. The children use scientific observation to note what happens when they try the different ball-ramp actions the teacher suggests (and think of themselves), and they discuss their findings with and report them to one another and the teacher (A). They use inference when they realize similarities, differences, and patterns among the different actions and what these mean, and they use prediction to answer the teacher's questions about "what would happen if..." before testing them by performing the suggested actions (C). They use measurement to calculate the height and length of the ramps, the speed at which the balls roll down them, the distance they roll, and they count the numbers of balls and ramps. And they use comparison (D) when they find the differences in the effects on speed and distance of varying ramp sizes, ramp numbers, ball numbers, etc.

81. B: Vibration is caused by anything physical moving rapidly back and forth. When an object vibrates, the vibrations disturb the medium surrounding it, which may be solid matter, liquids, or gases like the air. Sound does not cause vibrations in the air (A) but vice versa: vibrations are a type of energy. The sound caused by vibration is acoustic energy, and vibratory movements disturb their medium, like the air. Sound causes vibrations not only in the air, but also in the ear (C) when they reach it. Whereas sound waves traveling through the air and through the outer and middle ear are acoustic energy, once they reach the inner ear, it converts that acoustic energy into electrical energy that is sent via nerves to the brain (D).

82. A: The scientific method is a series of steps to solve a problem. Gathering information, asking scientific questions, and formulating hypotheses are all parts of the scientific method.

83. D: Living organisms change their behaviors according to internal cues, such as hunger, thirst, need for sunlight, need to reproduce, etc., and external cues like environmental changes, such as changes in temperature, amounts of water, availability of nutrients, etc. Their behavior is shaped NOT primarily by one or the other of these {(A), (B)} but by both. It is not controlled solely by genetic programming (C), but consists of adaptations to intrinsic needs and extrinsic changes in the environment.

Social Studies

84. C: In family systems theory, the family climate refers to the family's physical and emotional environment and emotional quality. Climate affects a child's feelings of safety or fear, support or rejection, and feeling loved or unloved. Hierarchy (A) refers to the family's balance of power, decision making, and control, which can change with changes in family makeup and is affected by factors like socioeconomic status, age, gender, religion, and culture. Boundaries (B) refer to the family's limits and definitions of togetherness and separateness, and what the family excludes or includes. Equilibrium (D) refers to the family's consistency or balance, which is preserved through family customs, traditions, and rituals, and disrupted by changes and stressors.

85. C: Lying at a little more than 23° south of the equator, the Tropic of Capricorn is the border between the Southern Temperate Zone to the south and the Tropical Zone to the north. The southern hemisphere is tilted toward the sun to its maximum extent each year at the winter solstice in December. The northernmost latitude at which the sun can appear directly overhead is at the Tropic of Cancer during the summer solstice. The northern and southern hemispheres are separated by the equator at 0° degrees latitude. The eastern and western hemispheres are separated by the prime meridian at 0° longitude.

86. C: There are no formal qualifications for members of the judicial branch. However, having a background in law is an informal qualification that is considered when appointing Article III judges.

87. B: In the early development of self-awareness, infants normally demonstrate eye-hand coordination by systematically reaching for and touching things they see by the age of 4 months (A). They regulate their reaching behaviors according to their physical sitting, posture, and balance levels by 4–6 months of age (C). They can typically tell the difference between video of themselves and of other babies dressed in identical clothing by the age of 6 months (D). They typically can tell the difference between live video of themselves and of others exactly mimicking their behaviors by the ages of 4–7 months (B).

88. D: Identification is the third of five progressive levels of self-awareness that children develop. In differentiation (B), the first level, children can distinguish their mirrored images from other people, and realize that their reflection's movements correspond to their own movements. In situation (C), the second level, children then realize their mirror images are unique to themselves and that their bodies and selves are situated in space. In identification (D), the third level, children identify their reflections as "me." When they see something on their reflected faces, they know to touch their faces rather than the mirror to touch or remove the object. In permanence (A), the fourth level, children realize their self is permanent over time and space, recognizing themselves in photos and videos regardless of their ages, clothing, location, etc. (The fifth level is self-consciousness or "meta"-self-awareness, i.e., seeing oneself from others' as well as one's own perspective.)

89. D: The scale would be largest on a map of Greenwich Village. Scale is described as large when it is closer to life-sized; the smaller the region being depicted, the closer to actual size the map can be. Of the four answer choices, Greenwich Village, a neighborhood in Manhattan, is the smallest. Therefore, it must be depicted in the largest scale. Incidentally, Benelux is the name for the region of northern Europe that includes Belgium, the Netherlands, and Luxembourg.

90. D: The only answer choice that represents a possible absolute location for New Orleans is 30° N, 90° W. When a location is described in terms of its placement on the global grid, it is customary to put the latitude before the longitude. New Orleans is north of the equator, so it has to be in the Northern Hemisphere. In addition, it is west of the prime meridian, which runs through Greenwich, England, among other places. So, New Orleans must be in the Western Hemisphere. It is possible, then, to deduce that 30° N, 90° W is the only possible absolute location for New Orleans.

91. A: Symbols are not used to represent relief on a physical map. A physical map is dedicated to illustrating the landmasses and bodies of water in a specific region, so symbols do not provide enough detail. Color, shading, and contour lines, on the other hand, are able to create a much more complicated picture of changes in elevation, precipitation, etc. Changes in elevation are known in geography as relief.

92. D: Individualistic cultures, like that of the United States, value scientific thinking and object manipulation as skills to teach young children. Individualism favors the independence of each person, individuals realizing their full potential (self-actualization), and distinguishing themselves from the group. Collectivism favors the interdependence (C) of individuals and their social relationships, interactions, and connections. Collectivist cultures value cooperation to achieve group harmony (B), while individualist cultures value competition among group members to achieve individual excellence.

93. B: Researchers have found that Hispanic families in the U.S. are more likely to choose home- and family-based child care and preschool education than outside centers. This may reflect the collectivist nature of Latin culture, which values social interactions and relationships more than structure. Caucasian parents in the U.S. are found to prefer preschool centers. This reflects not

Copyright © Mometrix Media. You have been licensed one copy of this document for personal use only. Any other reproduction or redistribution is strictly prohibited. All rights reserved.

only the North American culture's individualistic emphasis on structured early learning, and predominant North American custom, but also North American Caucasian parents' attention to scientific findings that center-based preschool education improves children's school readiness skills.

94. B: One factor educators must consider about immigrant parents is that they may not be aware of what special education and/or supplemental services are available to their children in American schools. Thus they are not negligent or refusing to request such services, but need to be informed about them, which educators must do. Culturally diverse parents and educators are likely to disagree about some educational goals for children, but educators should collaborate with parents to further those goals they both agree on rather than trying to convince parents to agree (A) on all goals. Educators should also remember that immigrant parents' not advocating for their children to receive needed services is not necessarily due to lack of interest (C) or resistance to confronting problems (D). In addition to lacking information, some parents from cultures with more paternalistic educational systems are trained *not* to speak up, but to wait for educators to raise concerns before expressing children's problems they have witnessed.

95. C: Research has found significant variations among parental age expectations for various EC developmental milestones (e.g., weaning, eating, toilet-training, dressing, sleeping, etc.). Thus what is normal for one culture is abnormal for another. For example, Anglo parents usually introduce and encourage drinking from a cup to one-year-olds, so an eighteen-month-old not doing this could signal some developmental delay; but Filipino parents normally have not even introduced a cup to eighteen-month-olds, so their not using cups is developmentally normal. As in this example, some developmental milestones not reached by a certain age is *not* always a cause for concern (D). Assessment data *are* more likely to be misinterpreted when the educators' and parents' cultures differ (A) than when they share a common culture. Although age expectations for milestones vary across cultures, educators *cannot* automatically attribute everything to this variation when a child could also need a complete developmental assessment (B).

96. D: Area differentiation in geography refers to regional variations in occupations. It also refers to regional variations in geographical characteristics; e.g., people grow different plants in highlands than in lowlands according to what grows best in their respective altitudes and climates. (A) is an example of the geographical concept of utility value, i.e., how much use natural resources are to different people—oceans have more utility value for fishermen than farmers, while forests have more utility value for naturalists than academics. (B) is an example of the geographical concept of spatial interrelatedness, i.e., the relationship of geographic phenomena and non-physical characteristics like rural or urban regions. (C) is an example of the geographical concept of agglomeration, i.e., the tendency of people and their settlements and activities to concentrate in the most profitable areas.

97. C: Physical geography focuses on processes and patterns in the natural environment. What people eat in any given geographic region is largely dependent on such environmental factors as climate and the availability of arable land. Religion, family, and language may all be affected by geographic factors, but they are not as immediately affected as dietary preferences.

98. A: In desert environments, where little rain falls, some animal species have adapted by estivating during the day, thus allowing the animals to escape the desert's searing daytime heat. The other answers can be eliminated because the associated climates are not nearly as hot, removing the impetus for an animal to avoid the daytime heat. The climate of a tundra, for example, is much cooler, and in that environment it would make much less sense for an animal to avoid daytime heat. This eliminates answer C. Options B and D can be rejected because the climates of the temperate forests and grasslands are not as hot as that of deserts, providing less reason for animals to adapt by estivating.

99. B: In order for students to understand causal relationships among historical events and processes, they must understand chronology. Analysis of historical succession patterns is a standard expected of high school students, not middle school students (A). However, students are expected to be able to interpret data from timelines by middle school, not high school (C). To instruct younger students in chronology, teachers *should* use narratives (D); e.g., histories written in story style, biographies, and historical literature. Such materials engage younger students' attention, help them to understand the historical motivations and actions of individuals and groups, and enable them to comprehend the relationships among antecedents, actions and events, and consequences as well as temporal event sequences.

100. B: Children's literature can not only be used to promote literacy and numeracy in young children; EC teachers also use it to teach civics concepts. (A) is incorrect. One reason is civics concepts become more real and concrete to young children when presented through stories whose situations children can understand (B). Another reason is young children can identify with or relate to characters in stories personally, making citizenship concepts thus delivered more relevant to them rather than distracting (C). EC teachers can also teach civics through a small-group activity wherein children write class rules, and then rewrite them more realistically (e.g., "No talking in class" becomes "Talk softly in class and listen when others talk"; "Stay in your seat" becomes "Sit down and go right to work"). This activity *will* teach civics ideas (D): through it, children come to understand judicial and legislative functions, and think about concepts like safety and fairness.

Arts

101. D: Assigning students to write an essay comparing and contrasting the influence that two famous American artists or artworks had on U.S. society would be most appropriate for helping high school students develop an appreciation for the value and role of art in U.S. society. The other activities mentioned, including having students create a slide show presentation about a famous American artist, asking students to create a timeline showing when famous works of American art were created, and taking students on a field trip to an art museum, would not necessarily achieve this learning goal because they do not include it explicitly.

102. D: Texture—rough, smooth, hard, soft, bumpy, slippery, etc.—is the element in art that affords the most tactile aesthetic experience to preschoolers. The art element of line (A) is more visual and has other benefits. Painting can be a tactile experience for preschoolers when they use finger paints, and even paintbrushes, but this does not pertain directly to color (B), which is visual, whereas texture is something better felt with fingers and hands by young children. Shape (C) can be felt by children in three-dimensional objects, but they also learn much about shapes through two-dimensional visual media. They learn more about textures by their feel in both three- and two-dimensional examples. Preschoolers can also learn to identify textures as represented visually in art, as they can do with lines, colors, and shapes; but among these four elements, texture is the one that lends itself most to tactile experiences.

103. C: Line is a very important element in visual art, but is not the best one to use to teach young children about three-dimensional shapes. For learning about 3-D shapes, EC teachers can better use the element of shape in art, because shape can be found in both 2-D (paintings, drawings, etc.) and 3-D (sculptures, mobiles, stabiles, etc.) artworks. While line is found in some form in nearly all visual art, it is easiest for young children to learn about it by examining two-dimensional drawings and paintings. Learning about line helps young children recognize more symbols (A); to develop their abilities to make comparisons (B); and to experiment with many different tools that can be used to draw lines (D), e.g., crayons, pencils, pens, markers, chalk, paint, etc.

104. A: The pitch of an individual note in music is determined by the frequency of the individual sound wave that produces that note. High-frequency sound waves produce high-pitched notes, middle frequencies produce medium-pitched notes, and low-frequency sound waves produce low-pitched notes. Particular frequencies equate to specific notes that have been assigned letter names in modern music, from A through G, with sharps and flats representing half-steps between notes. Tempo (B) is the relative speed at which music is played. Rhythm (C) includes time signature, i.e., the number of beats per measure; patterns among longer (held for more beats) and shorter (held for fewer beats) notes; and how notes are produced, like smoothly connected or *legato* vs. sharply disconnected or *staccato*. Harmony (D) is the combination of more than one note or pitch sounded at the same time, producing a pleasing effect. Two-part harmonies are commonly named by their intervals, e.g., thirds, fourths, fifths, sixths, etc. Harmonies with more than two parts are called chords.

105. B: EC aesthetic learning activities focusing on shapes help develop preschool children's abilities for forming concepts and early geometric math skills (A) as well as for creative thinking (C) and using their imaginations (B), and for being able to identify differences (D) between things. Identifying the properties of various shapes and how they differ helps with concept formation. Learning the names of shapes; whether they contain lines, angles, and/or arcs, what kinds, and how many; how shapes combine to form other shapes; and how shapes can be divided into other shapes, etc., helps with early geometry skills. Learning to manipulate shapes to create different forms and images stimulates creative thinking and using the imagination. And distinguishing among different shapes helps with identifying differences.

106. A: The most appropriate activity for students at this grade level would be making pinch pots and coil pots. Pinch pots are formed by creating a depression in the center of a ball of clay and smoothing the sides. Coil pots are formed by creating a long, thin length of clay and coiling it to form a pot. Unlike making and attaching handles to pots or throwing pots using a pottery wheel, creating this type of object with clay is appropriate given the fine motor skills and technical sophistication of second graders. The art teacher could model glazing pots using a kiln, but this activity would be too dangerous for young students to attempt on their own.

107. D: Form in visual art represents the three-dimensional projection of shape. It has dimension and volume; in three-dimensional artworks like sculptures, form has actual mass. In two-dimensional artworks like drawings and paintings, form does not have real mass; however, it can appear to have mass through the artist's visual techniques. Shapes in art may be positive, i.e., defined by outlines; or negative, i.e., defined only by the edges of surrounding shapes (A). Biomorphic shapes are shapes seen in nature. While some shapes found in nature can be geometric, like circles, ovals, and stars (e.g., starfish), many biomorphic shapes are not perfectly geometric or geometric at all (B). Value in visual art is not dependent on color (C); value means the range of lights and darks in the artwork, no matter what colors are or are not used.

108. A: An example of a preschool lesson to give children an aesthetic experience with color can begin by reading a children's story/singing a song about colors: involving other modalities helps integrate the element of color and the subject of visual arts into EC curriculum rather than isolating them (B). The teacher then shows children a painting or other artwork, which young children can appreciate on their own levels (C). Then the teacher presents a separate display of patches (square, round, etc.) of solid colors used in the painting/artwork, asking children to name these and other colors they know, and to name any colors in the painting not in the display. After this, the teacher should first demonstrate how to mix paints, and then give children paints in the three primary colors and have them see how many different colors they can create by mixing them differently. This exercise teaches preschoolers color names, and also sensory discrimination and classification (D).

109. C: Japanese bowls made for the traditional tea ceremony is an example of art that serves a physical purpose. Photography by Dorothea Lange, Gordon Parks, Arthur Rothstein, Walker Evans, and others, commissioned by the Farm Security Administration (FSA) during the Great Depression, showed the extreme poverty, hunger, and suffering of many people; this is an example of art that serves a social purpose. Da Vinci's "Last Supper" (B) painting, like many other artworks with religious themes, is an example of art that serves a personal purpose. Satire in art, like some of Goya's works (D), is an example of art that serves a social purpose.

110. A: In the process of creating art, the artist first imagines what ideas and feelings s/he wants to express. Then s/he plans how to do this by researching, experimenting with, and designing the materials and forms to use and how to work with them to accomplish the results desired. The artist then creates an artistic product, evaluates how effective it is and how satisfied s/he is with it, and refines the product based on the evaluation. Once the artist is satisfied with the product, s/he then presents it to an audience of others who can participate with and respond to it.

Health and Physical Education

111. A: Through engaging in physical activity, children learn to expend physical and mental effort and to persevere when they encounter difficulty. These experiences not only enhance their self-esteem, i.e., feeling and thinking well of themselves, but also their self-efficacy, i.e., their feeling that they are competent to perform specific tasks. Children's motor skills typically develop younger than their language skills, not vice versa (B); hence physical activity is an important way for them to express themselves before they can do so verbally. Children not only develop their motor skills through participating in physical games and sports; they also learn social skills (C) from interacting with peers and adults during these activities. Children not only enjoy the social interaction; normally, young children naturally seek out physical activity (D) and get pleasure from physical movement.

112. D: Children's motor skills normally develop the fastest between the ages of two and six years. From birth to four years (A), infants lift their heads and control their eye muscles; then learn to roll over and grasp; then sit up and crawl; stand and creep by one year; learn to walk, then run, kick, jump; and by three to four years can jump up and down and stand on one leg. By five years (B), they typically can skip, broad-jump, and dress themselves. By six to seven years (C), they are skillful with throwing, catching, dodging, and directing balls, and can tie their shoelaces and color pictures.

113. B: The WHO's recommendations are that young people engage in at least one hour per day of aerobic activity, which strengthens the heart, lungs, and large muscle groups. This makes the cardiovascular and respiratory systems more efficient in the absorption and transportation of oxygen. These recommendations also include at least three sessions a week of weight-bearing activity, which strengthens the bones.

114. C: The NASPE has developed six national standards for physical education. While certainly it is good for children as well as adults to consider their diets in conjunction with physical activity for physical fitness, the NASPE's standards are focused specifically on physical *education* and hence do not address diet. The criteria included in these standards *do* directly mention health (A): the third of six standards is that a physically educated individual reaches and sustains a physical fitness level that enhances his or her health. They also *do* mention self-respect as well as social interaction as benefits (B): the fifth standard states that a physically educated individual shows behaviors reflecting self-respect and respect for others within the contexts of physical activity. These standards also *do* mention pleasure (D): the sixth standard is that the physically educated person values the benefits of physical activities, which include pleasure as well as improving and maintaining health; offering physical, personal, and social challenges; and opportunities to express oneself and interact socially with others.

115. B: According to research by the Institute of Medicine (2013), more physically active children can focus their attention better than children who are less active (A). Children who get more exercise show better performance on standardized academic tests (B). More physical activity also improves children's working memory (C) and their problem-solving skills (D).

116. B: It is recommended that 20 to 35 percent of total calorie consumption should be from fats; 45 to 65 percent of total calories should be carbohydrates; and 10 to 35 percent should be protein.

117. B: Isotonic muscle contractions involve tension and changes in the length of the muscles in response to tension. Isotonic contractions consist of two types – eccentric and concentric. Eccentric is where the muscle lengthens against a resistance force. An example of this would be walking down stairs where the muscles need to lengthen in order to lower the individual's body weight. Concentric is the opposite and this is where the muscles are shortened such as walking up the stairs where the muscles must contract in order to lift the body weight. Other examples of concentric movement are sit ups, throwing a ball and raising the body up from a squatting position.

118. A: Cardiac output is total volume of blood that is pumped by the heart over a certain period of time. This value is typically reported in the number of liters per minute. Cardiac output is determined by the product of heart rate and stroke volume. Heart rate is the number of heart beats per minute and stroke volume is the amount of blood that is pumped by the left ventricle in each heart beat or contraction. A typical heart can pump approximately 5 liters of blood per minute. As the intensity of exercise increases, the cardiac output can increase as high as 40 liters per minute. An individual's heart rate will increase linearly until the maximum level is reached. Stroke volume, however, tends to increase to approximately 40-50% of the maximum and will then level off. Aerobic exercise helps to strengthen the heart, pump blood more efficiently and increase stroke volume.

119. A: A child with Attention Deficit Hyperactivity Disorder (ADHD) who becomes exhausted from engaging in excessive physical activity is an example of an emotional (and behavioral) condition that can affect levels of physical activity and fitness. A child with depression who avoids physical activity is also an example of this. The need to monitor a child with asthma for breathing problems during exercise (B) is an example of how a physical factor can affect physical activity and fitness levels, as are the need to monitor the exercise of a child with diabetes and coordinate it with the child's diet (C), and a physically disabled child's need for adaptive equipment (and/or alternative instructional methods) to participate in physical activities (D).

120. C: Rhythmic activities like dance and creative movements help students learn to control their bodies. While music is often used, the primary goal is body control. Locomotor, non-locomotor, and manipulative movements are used during rhythmic activities which can aid in the performance of skills, like gymnastics or dance routines.

Thank You

We at Mometrix would like to extend our heartfelt thanks to you, our friend and patron, for allowing us to play a part in your journey. It is a privilege to serve people from all walks of life who are unified in their commitment to building the best future they can for themselves.

The preparation you devote to these important testing milestones may be the most valuable educational opportunity you have for making a real difference in your life. We encourage you to put your heart into it—that feeling of succeeding, overcoming, and yes, conquering will be well worth the hours you've invested.

We want to hear your story, your struggles and your successes, and if you see any opportunities for us to improve our materials so we can help others even more effectively in the future, please share that with us as well. **The team at Mometrix would be absolutely thrilled to hear from you!** So please, send us an email (support@mometrix.com) and let's stay in touch.

If you feel as though you need additional help, please check out the other resources we offer:

Study Guide: http://MometrixStudyGuides.com/PraxisII

Flashcards: http://MometrixFlashcards.com/PraxisII